A SHORT BREAK IN BUDAPEST

NCQ TITLES

Legal Fictions
Politics & Letters
On Yeats: Upon a House
Drama & Democracy
Locating Theology

Time Pieces
Critical Paranoia
On Joyce: 3 easy essays
On Eliot
Literary Conversions

Film-texts

A Trip to Rome
A Short Break in Budapest
Magic in Prague

A Week in Venice
Four Days in Athens
The Last Priest of Horus

WWW: the weekend that warped the world

Play-texts

Darwin: an evolutionary entertainment
Strange Meetings & Shorts

Eliotics

Forthcoming

Rubbishing Hockney & other reviews
On Collecting Walter Benjamin
Autobiography & Class Consciousness
Considering Canterbury Cathedral

*Though each can be read independently,
these NCQ publications, taken together,
comprise a single hyper-text collection.*

A SHORT BREAK
IN BUDAPEST

a film-text

Bernard Sharratt

New Crisis Quarterly
2015

NEW CRISIS QUARTERLY
ncq@newcrisisquarterly.myzen.co.uk

First published 2015

ISBN : 978-1-910956-12-0

For Péter & Àgnes
(with apologies for the Hungarian)

and

in homage to
John Berger

I am grateful to John Berger for permission to use material from *Jonah Who will be 25 in the Year 2000* and to Cevat Çapan for arranging that permission.

© Bernard Sharratt 2015

This film-text is not written with actual film production in mind. Though it plays with a variety of film genres, it is primarily intended to be read—and imagined.

Budapest is an appropriate place as the setting for my characters and my themes, and the script is designed to be easily supplemented by on-line images and maps of the specified sites and scenes around Budapest and Lake Balaton. Other film-texts in this 'city' series are set in Athens, Prague, Rome, and Venice, and the series will probably conclude with *A Last Sight of Europe*.

A film-text is a particularly suitable form for the New Crisis Quarterly imprint, since that name revives the title of a very short-lived periodical, whose first, only, and final issue appeared in 1984, under the guise of my *The Literary Labyrinth*. Its editorial programme was to publish reviews of imagined books I didn't feel I had the time actually to write, so its readers were cheerfully invited, if so inclined, to write those works themselves. In the same spirit, reading a film-text means that most of the work of imagining the film can be done by you, which is part of the fun of writing them.

B.S.
2015

CREDITS OVER:]

1. TRAIN SEQUENCE:

Brief shots from various train windows of stations across Europe: Bruxelles and Lille at night, leaving Köln in early morning, then Munich, Vienna.
Passing station announcements audible in various languages.

Intercut with :
brief shots of PAUL seated at a window in successive carriages. Paul is maybe 25, personable, but not very confident of himself.

Brief shots of Paul writing desultorily on a laptop; reading a Hungarian phrase book, mouthing phrases; dozing; gazing out of windows: Cologne cathedral, Rhine views at dusk, lights reflected in windows, landscapes passing.

Sequence ends with departure from Vienna station.

END CREDITS]

Written:] SUNDAY.

2. INT. TRAIN CARRIAGE. LATE AFTERNOON.

Paul finally finishes typing, closes laptop, and looks up to the Hungarian sign for 'restaurant car' at rear of train, one carriage away. He counts some money, shrugs. Hesitates about taking the laptop with him but then decides to do so.

He makes his way to the restaurant car and is about to enter when he collides in the doorway with LEA as she exits from the WC in the space between carriages.
Paul drops his laptop and they both bend down for it, clashing heads as they do so.
She picks up the laptop and hands it to him.
He is embarrassed at his awkwardness, she is very self-confident.

Lea is mid-twenties, very attractive, dressed in casual student-type clothes, with a brilliant smile, but wary.

>PAUL
>I'm terribly sorry. *(pidgin Hungarian:)*
>Er, kosunum? Saj-nalom.

>LEA
>*(almost perfect English)*
>You're welcome. *(corrects his pronunciation:)*
>KO-sunum—is how we say it.

They are both awkwardly in the doorway to the restaurant car. Paul is much taken with Lea, but unsure of himself and of his non-Hungarian.

>PAUL
>You speak English?
>*(He notices the interior of lovely old restaurant carriage and reacts:)* That's beautiful!

>LEA.
>Well, it's useful. *(i.e. speaking English is)*

>PAUL
>Sorry, I meant: the restaurant car. It's lovely. Old-fashioned.

>LEA
>If it's old, that only means they cannot afford to replace it. Yet.

>PAUL
>Oh, I see. That's a pity. *(entangles himself)*
>Well, no, not quite. Er, I was going to get some coffee, or lunch. Perhaps you could help me—with the menu, I mean. I don't speak Hungarian.

LEA
(amused at the clumsy pass) The menu will be in
Hungarian, German, French —and English.
(She slides past him to get into the restaurant car.)

PAUL
But—

LEA
(glances back teasingly)
And the Hungarian for coffee is: Kave.
And the Hungarian for goodbye is búcsú.
Or: viszontlátásra. *(smiles sweetly)* Búcsú.

She enters and sits at a table. He enters and sits near, but not at the same table. A few other passengers are scattered in the car.

WAITER arrives. Lea orders coffee and a pastry in Hungarian.

PAUL *(to Waiter)*
Er, Kave, er, kerem.

WAITER *(very good English)*
How would you like your coffee, sir? With milk?
Cappucino? Expresso? Black? With sugar? Without?

PAUL
Er, with milk. No, er, Expresso, thank you.
And the menu, please.

Waiter points to the menu, which is already on the table, and leaves. Mildly flustered, Paul reads the menu while keeping half an eye on Lea, who is perfectly conscious that he is looking at her and is quite enjoying both the attention and his discomfort.

Waiter returns with a coffee.

PAUL
I'll have the goulash stew, please.
Or goulash soup, I should say, yes?

Waiter leaves. Paul starts drinking coffee, while still eyeing Lea covertly.

     P.A.
  [*Longish train announcement in rapid Hungarian. Not pre-recorded. No translation* :] Van egy akadály a pályán. Ez a vonat megszűnik a következő állomást. Megpróbáljuk intézi a szállítást a további le a pályáról. Ott lesz késedelem néhány órát.

The other passengers react as if the announcement is both important and irritating.

     PAUL
  (looks across pleadingly to Lea)
  Er, what is the Hungarian for Help!

     LEA
  Yes, I think you will need help.
  (She hesitates, then gets up and joins him at the table, bringing her coffee). I will join you.

     PAUL
  Please do. *(stands awkwardly in politeness)*
  I'm Paul. *(she sits, he sits)*

Lea does not give her name. She explains the announcement:

     LEA
  There is an obstacle, yes? On the line. A fallen tree. The train will stop at the next station and we will probably all get on a bus.

     PAUL
  To Budapest?

     LEA
  No, to the station after the obstacle. Then we wait for another train for Budapest.

PAUL
Will there be a long delay? You see, I am being met by, er, someone at Budapest train station. And I don't know how to alert them.

LEA.
I will find out. *(slight tease)* And who, Mr Paul, is meeting you at Budapest?

PAUL
Er, nobody. Er, personal. That is. I'm supposed to be met by, well, a sort of official, y'know.

LEA
Ah, you are sort of official, yes?

Lea doesn't wait for his denial, but goes off to find information.

WAITER *(comes over to Paul)*
We are sorry, sir. It is too late to prepare your goulash. It would not be ready before we stop. You understand, sir. Sorry.

PAUL
That's OK. I understand. Kosunum.

Lea is talking to the few other passengers in the car. Paul looks anxious. She returns.
The train is starting to slow down.

LEA.
It is *un peu compliqué*. The train will stop soon. The bus will take perhaps one half-hour, but there will be a long wait for another train at the next station. We will not be in Budapest for at least two hours, they say. Some passengers plan to take taxis all the way. It is not *too* far to Budapest.

PAUL
We could share a taxi —if you like.
I'm sure the British Council will pay.

LEA
Perhaps. If we can find a taxi. But why would
the British Council pay for your taxi?

PAUL
Well, I'm their guest, sort of—
That's who's supposed to be meeting me.
I'm giving a talk at the Petőfi Museum tomorrow.
For the anniversary of the 1956, er, uprising.
Sort of. *(a favourite, nervous phrase)*

LEA *(surprised)*
You are a historian of Hungary? *(pause)*
And you do not speak Hungarian?

PAUL
No, not at all. No. I teach English literature.
In England. Well, sort of. I used to.
They asked me to give a talk about a British writer
—who wrote a novel about the 1956 events, sort of.
It's a bit *compliqué*.

LEA
So why are you travelling by train?—
if the British Council is paying your expenses.
It is a long way from England to Budapest by train.

PAUL
Well, to be honest, I bought a Euro-Rail Pass with
the British Council money—instead of a plane
ticket —so I can have some free travelling around
afterwards. You see, I'm actually out of a job at the
moment, and it's a cheap way to get a holiday.
And I thought by train I might meet a little
adventure along the way. Er, and what do you do?

                    LEA
          Mmm. *(teasing)* Well, Mr Paul, I am not
          a little adventure 'along the way'.

Paul is mortified at his faux pas. She smiles and continues.

                    LEA
          I work as a tourist guide. I am a very good,
          what do you say, girl guide:
          I can show you all the famous sights of Budapest—
          in twenty minutes flat.

                    PAUL
          I'd be delighted to have you—as a, er, girl guide.
          If I could afford it, I'd pay you with pleasure.

                    LEA *(teasing, drily)*
          Thank you, Mr Paul, but I would prefer money.

                    PAUL
          (another faux pas) I didn't mean—

The train is audibly and quickly coming to a stop.

                    LEA
          (looks out of window, at station in view)
          We need to get our luggage. Now.
          I will see you on the platform. Yes?

They leave—Paul just remembering to leave some money on the table for the coffees.

3. EXT. TRAIN STATION FORECOURT.

*Outside a small train station. Chaos as people pile off the train.
There are only three taxis and they are rapidly filling up. Lea has gone
ahead fast and has managed to secure the one last seat in a taxi.
Gestures to Paul who is guarding both sets of (not much) luggage.*

LEA
There is only one seat. You must take it.

PAUL
No, no, I insist. You take it.

LEA
But *I* speak Hungarian. And you do not.
I can wait for the train.
And the Great British Council are not awaiting me. . .

PAUL *(smiles)*
You could sit on my lap—

LEA *(smiles)*
No, Mr Paul, but thank you for your kind offer.
Now, go, before you lose your seat.

PAUL
But how do I see you again—to thank you?

LEA
Budapest is a small city. You never know, Mr Paul,
I may perhaps turn up at your lecture.
At the Petőfi Museum, tomorrow?

PAUL
But I don't even know your name,

LEA
Olah Lea.

PAUL *(squeezes into crowded taxi)*
What is the Hungarian for *au revoir*, Olah?

LEA *(smiles and waves him away)*
Au revoir.

4. TAXI SEQUENCE.

Brief and rapid sequence of frantically fast taxi drive along minor roads, with Paul crushed into a small battered taxi with extremely voluble Hungarian passengers, none of whom speak English. They are mainly complaining.

Large middle-aged female taxi driver. Hair-raising ride.

5. EXT. KELETI STATION. NEARLY DUSK.

Taxi arrives outside Budapest Keleti station. All tumble out. Each pays taxi driver till Paul is the only one left. It's about 8 pm.

> TAXI DRIVER *(in Hungarian)*
> Ön részesedés 5,100 forints.
> *(your share is 5,100 forints — 15 pounds).*
> *(She realises he doesn't understand so holds up two hands, with 5 fingers and 1 finger)*

Paul nods as if he's understood, but he hasn't. He takes out his nearly empty wallet and hands over one 5-thousand and one 10-thousand forint note. Taxi driver registers this, then she hands back the 5K note and 4,900 forints in various change from the 10K note.
Paul is utterly confused, till she points to the '10' on the 10K note—comparing it with the '1' on a one-thousand note. Paul nods gratefully. Taxi speeds away.

6. EXT. KELETI STATION. DUSK.

Paul wheels his travel-case into the main part of the station and looks around for his contact.

Man approaches him : ANDREW BRADLEY, about 60, British Council rep, old pro. Near retirement. Denholm Elliot type. Efficient, reasonably friendly, used to talking without bothering to listen much. Impatient. Talks fast.

                    ANDREW
            Dr. Paul Connor? Thought I recognised you.
            (Paul is puzzled). They e-mail us digital photos.
            All very hi-tech. Makes life easier I suppose,
            when you're constantly meeting total strangers.
            I'm Bradley, Andrew Bradley. British Council.
            Glad you made it. Gather the Vienna train was
            delayed.

                    PAUL
            Yes, indeed. I'm afraid I had to take a taxi.
            Er, on expenses, I hope? *(No response to this from
            Bradley)* But many thanks for waiting for me.
            Hope it hasn't been too much of a hassle.

                    ANDREW
            (walks him smartly out of the station)
            Well, Keleti Station isn't my idea of heaven.
             So let's get you out of it. We're running pretty late.
            Should be at dinner in thirty minutes. But I'll have
            to get you booked into the Gellert beforehand.
            Got another engagement later, I'm afraid.
            So, just time to give you my quickie Budapest tour
            on the way. Twenty minutes flat.
            Get you orientated. You OK with your luggage?
            (Does not offer to help). Car's this way.

7. CAR SEQUENCE.

In car : views of the city. Brief shots, rapid sequence: the route is from Keleti towards the river and then over river and up Gellert Hill to panoramic spot overlooking the Danube.

Andrew drives fast and talks fast along the way, filling Paul in: a well-practised and peremptory routine.

Paul peers out of the window eagerly at passing sights.

ANDREW *(as he drives)*
Right, we're heading over to the river. Danube, of course. Though blue it isn't, these days. This side is Pest, flat, all the way back to the plains. Other side is Buda, the hilly bits. Buda-Pest. Combined in the 1870s. Things used to go in two's in this part of the world. Austro-Hungarian. Dual monarchy. Two capitals. Vienna, Budapest. Though Budapest got the short end of things usually. There'll be a map and tourist handbook for you in your room. You can mug up on the history.

PAUL
Well, I do know a bit of it, of course. '56 for a start.

ANDREW
Sorry. Of course. Most Brits who come here, even for us, haven't a clue about the place. Now, passing over the Szabadsag Bridge, 'Freedom Bridge', one of three main ones—
up there, the monstrous Liberty statue.
Not to everybody's taste. Originally supposed to have a propellor in her hand. Poor lass—
Was supposed to commemorate the '45 Soviet Liberation. Since '89, just called 'Liberty', of course. Whatever that means. Right, brief stop, Gellert Hill. Best views in town. Come and get your bearings.

8. EXT. GELLERT HILL. DUSKISH.

They get out of the car at the top of Gellert Hill and walk over to the panoramic view. Stunning evening. Paul is genuinely impressed.

ANDREW *(rapidly pointing:)*
OK, Buda on this bank: hills, Castle, St Michael's Church, old town. All of it restored after the war. Rubble in '45. Thanks partly to us, of course.
(Paul looks surprised) We bombed it flat. Well, they've done a decent job of restoring it, I must say. Back there is Pest, flat-land. Houses of Parliament there,

Saint Stephen's Basilica with the dome, the Petőfi Museum is just over there *(points)*, where you'll be lecturing tomorrow. Straight across the bridge here and turn *left* at Kalvin Square. And we're eating over there *(points)*—Raday Streeet. Turn *right* at Kalvin Square. Can't miss it. Got the general picture? Very easy place to find your way around— in Pest the main boulevards form concentric half-circles, and all cross-roads lead to the river. Or away from it, of course. Three main bridges. Impossible to get lost.

    PAUL
I'll try not to. *(pauses in admiration)*
It's a very beautiful city.

    ANDREW
Indeed. *(as they quickly get back into car and take the short ride to Gellert Hotel:)* OK, let's get you to the Gellert. Grand hotel, old style. Hideously expensive these days, but the BC has had a deal with them from the old days —good discount—not much longer, I'm afraid, so enjoy it while it lasts. And the Gellert has the best Turkish Baths in town—though they *are* expensive— and *not* part of your deal, I'm afraid. So it's up to you, and your wallet, if you want to indulge. Though you can always have a go at the paddling pool, with the famous wave-machine. That's thrown in with the B&B, I gather—Done a lot of these British Council overseas jaunts?

    PAUL
Not unless you count Wales.

    ANDREW
(brief pause, laughs)
Ah, yes, I remember that story.
Right, here we are.

9. INT. GELLERT HOTEL FOYER.

> ANDREW *(as Paul checks in.)*
> OK, dinner this evening. Our hosts are Gábor Könyves from the Institute of Literature, Academy of Sciences, and Anna Kelemen, from the Petőfi. Full title: Petőfi Museum for the History of Hungarian Literature. Strange to have a museum of literature, but this is Hungary. Half the streets in Budapest are named after writers. Right, you have a quick wash and brush up, and I'll be on the terrace—through there *(points)*. Just time for a gin and tonic. Ten minutes? I'll ring and ask them to hold dinner a bit longer. Hungry?
>
> PAUL
> Actually, I'm absolutely starving. I didn't even manage to get lunch on the train. So I've only had a croissant since yesterday.
>
> ANDREW
> Well, the Hungarians are famous eaters. In fact, the main puzzle about the Hungarian economy these days is how it ever manages to feed the enormous appetites of the Hungarians. Huge quantities. And the food is superb. You'll enjoy it.

12. EXT. DINING AREA ON THE STREET OUTSIDE A RESTAURANT. BALMY EVENING.

At the (e.g.) Vorosposatakocsi Restaurant in Raday Street, one of many along both sides of the street. The street is very busy with locals and tourist diners. Cheerful noisy atmosphere. Getting dark.
But this restaurant is oddly empty and a major row is clearly going on in the kitchen area at the back of the restaurant. Voices raised in anger. And from the restaurant balcony above, sounds of a few raucous English yobs, loudly singing Chelsea football chants.

Seated at a front table in the restaurant's almost empty seating enclosure on the pavement are GÁBOR and ANNA, looking anxious. They rise to greet Andrew and Paul as they arrive.

          ANDREW
     Anna *(kisses hand)*, Gábor, *(shakes hand).*
     This is Paul Connor, your guest lecturer tomorrow.

General hand-shaking, but everybody distracted by the audible row.

          GÁBOR
     (In very good and very careful English, soft-spoken, some
     hesitation in order to be exact. Gábor is a gentle giant.)
     I am afraid that we have a little problem.
     I chose this restaurant for you because the owner is
     a very good friend and I knew we would have an
     excellent meal. But Georgy is having some
     difficulties this evening.
     And I am not sure what we should do.

An irate chef suddenly storms out past them.

          GEORGY
     (follows the chef, expostulating in Hungarian, but gives up and
     comes over and greets them. In fairly basic English.)
     Gábor's friends. I am very happy to welcome you.
     But Gábor will tell you, yes. We have problems.

          GÁBOR
     Georgy's waiters have all suddenly walked out on
     him. And now his chef too. In the middle of the
     evening serving. They suddenly demanded to be
     paid large extra bonuses, immediately, right now.
     He said he could not possibly do that.
     It is Sunday evening. The banks are not open.
     He has not enough cash. And they have given him
     no warning. He is—devastated.

          GEORGY *(distressed)*
     I do not know why this. I am a good boss. Why?

ANNA
(also good English, though would often prefer French)
Most of his customers have now gone elsewhere —
there is much competition, after all.
(She indicates the rest of the very busy street.)

GÁBOR
But Georgy says he can still serve us a basic cold
meal—some melon, ham, cheese. It will not be the
magnificent feast I had hoped for you.
But I would not like to 'let him down'.
I would feel I was betraying him. You understand?

ANDREW *(gracious and cheerful)*
Not at all, Gábor. So long as there's good
Hungarian wine to drink, and your good selves
are here. Not a problem. Though we are late,
and I do have an Embassy party to get to,
fairly soon, so—

GEORGY
(speaks rapidly in Hungarian to Gábor :)
*[Ezek az angol huligánok - követelik a dara, és nem
hajlandók elhagyni. És ők részegek. Tudna segíteni?]*

GÁBOR *(explains:)*
There is another problem. Upstairs. Those English
boys—they demand their full meal, which he can no
longer serve, and they refuse to leave or to pay.
They are trouble. And they are drunk. So, can we help?

*Drunken singing and loud chants of 'Chelsea! Chelsea!' from above,
getting more and more raucous.*

ANDREW *(quickly)*
I rather think we'd better not get involved with that,
Gábor.

Gábor looks uncertain what to do. Georgy is still at their table, but anxious.

A customer comes across from another table, where three men are still sitting : BORIS, IVAN, *and* DIMITRI.

VOROSHENSKY *is a large heavily built man in his late fifties, with a distinctly military bearing.*

Voroshensky addresses Georgy in Russian.

> VOROSHENSKY
> (Mogu li ya pomoch? Ya dolzhen moi vengerskiye druz'ya odolzheniye. Ya nakhodilsya zdes' v kachestve soldat - do 1989 A ya ne lyublyu Angliyskiye khuligany . Ya "govorit" s nimi.)

Georgy nods.

Gábor understands the Russian and translates for Paul and Andrew.

> GÁBOR
> Now this might be, shall we say—interesting. The Russian gentleman here is offering to help. He says he owes his Hungarian friends a favour! Which is perhaps only too true. He says he was stationed here as a soldier—before 1989.
> And Colonel Voroshensky says he does not like 'English hooligans'. He will 'talk' to them, he says. But —he will need me to translate into English for him. So I will see what I can do!

> ANDREW
> Are you sure that's wise, Gábor?

> GÁBOR
> Georgy is a very old friend. I should help, if I can.

Led by Colonel Voroshensky, the four burly Russians proceed into the interior of the restaurant, with Georgy and Gábor following.
They all head for the stairs to the upstairs room.

On the way two Russians pick up large knives from the kitchen area. Camera stays with the front table.

> ANDREW *(to Paul)*
> We most definitely keep out of this one, I suggest.

> ANNA
> *(smiles uneasily, then, as a deliberately poor joke, to Paul)*
> I do hope you are enjoying your very first visit to Hungary, Paul.

> PAUL
> Well, it has not been *quite* what I expected. So far.

There are sounds of crashes from upstairs and the chanting suddenly stops. Shouting in Russian. Swearing in English. Then howls of pain. Three scruffy English 20-year-olds climb rapidly down the outside of the balcony, using the drainpipes and ornamental stonework, almost falling over themselves in fright.
But as they reach the street they look semi-defiantly up.
Voroshensky appears on the balcony and says something contemptuously to them in Russian.
Gábor beside him translates to the yobs in the street:

> GÁBOR
> The Colonel says: He will tell his good friend Mr Abramovitch that you are a disgrace to the Chelsea Football team.

> YOBS *(variously)*
> Fuck Off! Bollocks! Fucking Ruskies!
> Chelsea! Chelsea! Chelsea!

But they leave rapidly, down the street, shouting, and nursing hurt arms and faces.

> ANDREW
> "Exit pursued by a bear . . ."

Andrew, Anna and Paul watch them go, as the Russians, Georgy and Gábor reappear downstairs. In the background Georgy shakes hands with the Russians and thanks them warmly (in Russian-Hungarian). The Russians refuse Georgy's offer of free drinks, and insist on leaving. But a brief conversation first, in Russian, with Gábor and Georgy.

The four Russians leave —in the same direction as the yobs.
Gábor rejoins the group at the table.
Georgy goes off to get wine and food.
Rest of the restaurant is now completely empty and Georgy puts up a Closed sign, though Gábor's group is still at their table.

> GÁBOR
> Indeed, that *was* most interesting.
> Colonel Voroshensky says that he recognises the pattern of tonight. He has seen it before, he says—in Russia. He has told Georgy that the restaurant will probably receive a phone call tomorrow—from someone who will offer to give him 'protection' against 'labour troubles'—like waiters who suddenly walk off the job.

> ANNA
> And from tourists who make drunken trouble?

> PAUL
> You mean the whole thing was staged?

> GÁBOR
> Possibly. We will see. There are criminal gangs who try to control businesses in Hungary. Protection rackets. This was perhaps a 'warning'?

> ANNA
> If they control the bars and restaurants, it also allows them to fiddle the credit cards of foreign tourists. Or they charge large amounts, put an extra zero on the bill, and few tourists realise the scam.

GÁBOR
And they can also even clone the credit cards for
fraud. It is a growing racket. They steal identities,
is that how you put it?

ANDREW *(changing the subject)*
Well, let's put it all behind us now. It seems to be over,
anyway. Let's have some good Hungarian wine,
at least. And perhaps just something to nibble, eh.

GÁBOR
Yes, Georgy would be most upset if we left now.
But I think we have just a little to eat. Paul, I am so
sorry this has happened. It is not normally like this.

ANNA *(trying to normalise the evening)*
And we were looking forward to hearing about your
lecture for tomorrow. You are talking mainly about
John Berger's novel about 1956, yes?

Georgy arrives with plates of bread, cheese, ham, bottles of wine.

PAUL
*(glancing enviously at customers in nearby restaurants being
served huge helpings of marvellously cooked hot food—)*
And about time—

GEORGY *(hearing this, and a bit hurt)*
I am sorry. For the delay.

PAUL
*(horrified at yet another faux pas—tries to obliterate it by
talking fast:)* No, no. Not at all. What I was saying
was that my *talk* tomorrow will be *about* time.
It's one of John Berger's themes, and the notion of
time seemed appropriate for an anniversary. So I'm
going to talk about time and history in his work.
The novel is called *A Painter of Our Time*, after all.
(he is about to get started on his topic—)

ANDREW
(interrupts, changing the topic, away from serious content)
Well, time enough for that tomorrow, eh.
(as they start to drink and nibble at the food) (jokingly:)
You do realise, Paul, that you're being here is itself a bit of an identity theft? Or mistaken identity, at least. *(explains to Gábor and Anna)* When we were asked for a speaker for this anniversary of the '56 events, somebody did a search on the British Council's nice new computerised data-base, and Paul's name came up with a 'Buda' tag—but it turned out this didn't mean Buda-pest at all. Apparently, you gave a talk on *Buddhism* at one of our literary conferences, yes? And our data people can't spell Buddha.
But then they saw that you'd actually done your PhD on John Berger and it seemed you fitted the bill after all. So here you are. *(mild laughter)*

ANNA
So you are a Buddhist, Paul?

PAUL *(embarrassed)*
(He has barely managed to get a bite to eat and is now reluctantly drawn into talking rather than eating)
No, no—not at all. That was actually another daft mistake. I'd agreed to do a paper for a conference, in Wales, and the secretary rang me, on a bad phone line, to ask for a title, and I said: Oh, just call it 'Marxism and Criticism'—but she mis-heard me and I was advertised as talking about 'Buddhism and Criticism'. I was actually introduced by the chairman as about to talk on that title.
It was all pretty embarrassing.

GÁBOR *(laughing)*
Well, these days there are probably more Buddhists than Marxists in our country! Perhaps you should talk about Buddhism after all.

PAUL *(changing the topic, to Andrew)*
So, am I the only British Council speaker for this
anniversary occasion? And I'm a sort of mistake?

ANDREW *(looking at his watch)*
Well, general cut-backs and all that.
We've all got to economise. So I'm afraid the only
other Brit contribution is a local ex-pat—
a photographer who was actually here in '56,
took some famous shots of the rising.
He's been living here since '89.
We're sponsoring a book launch for him,
on Wednesday. You'll meet him tomorrow.

GÁBOR
I'm afraid even the commemoration of 1956 itself is
a little controversial these days. So this is just a small
occasion, to mark the end of a temporary exhibition
that opened on the actual anniversary.

ANDREW
Now, if it's OK with everybody, I really must be
going to that embassy party. Paul, you'll be OK
finding your way back to the Gellert?
I showed you the way. It's only across the bridge.

ANNA *(concerned)*
We could walk with you, Paul, if you like.
Yes, Gábor?

GÁBOR *(awkwardly)*
Well, Anna, I think I had better see if Georgy has
any more trouble, it's difficult—

PAUL
No, no, please, both of you. Wouldn't dream of it.
No. I can easily find my way. No problem.
*(He has stood up and realises that he is now committed to
leaving—even though he has barely eaten at all.)*
—Er, and tomorrow?

ANNA
Ah, yes. If you come to the Petőfi Museum at 11, I can show you around, and give you some lunch before your lecture at one. Would that suit?

ANDREW *(in a hurry, not very helpfully)*
Right, Paul, just give me a ring if you have any problems. I'll be at the British Council office in the morning. The Petőfi is on your map, it's easy enough to get to. Just over the river.
Now I really *must* dash. I'll point you on your way, if you like. 'Bye everybody.

General leaving, shaking of hands etc.
Andrew vaguely gestures Paul in the right direction.

PAUL
That's fine. I'll be fine. No, please—*(he gestures at Gábor and Anna to stay, and then leaves quickly.)* Goodbye! —Er, búcsú ?

13. EXT. KELVIN SQUARE AREA. DARK.

Brief sequence: Paul is walking in the Kelvin Square area, trying to find somewhere still open to eat at, but he looks at several menu prices and thinks better of it. Wanders briefly about, avoiding skate-boarders etc., then tries to find his way out of the square towards the Gellert Hotel, but is now unsure of the right direction. Goes to a taxi rank and asks a taxi-driver:

PAUL *(laboriously)*
Beszél angolul, kérem?
(Do you speak English, please?)

TAXI DRIVER
Sure thing buddy. Three years in New York.

PAUL
Er, how much to the Gellert Hotel?

                    TAXI DRIVER
The Gellert? *(brief pause, then gambles :)*
Well, it's after ten, so I have to charge double.
And we can only use the northern bridge at this
time of night. That makes it the long way round.
So, it's going to be, say, eight thousand Hungarian.
Or 25 dollars US if you have it. In advance.

                    PAUL *(grins)*
Sure. I'm not a *total* mug, you know, mate.

                    TAXI-DRIVER.
Well, if you can afford the Gellert, it was worth a
try!

                    PAUL
Fair enough. But I *can't* afford the Gellert.
Long story. So, where's the nearest bridge? I'll walk.

                    TAXI-DRIVER *(cheerful)*
That-a-way. Ten minutes max.

                    PAUL
Better luck next time.

14. EXT. DARK. WALK-WAY ON BRIDGE.

Paul starting to walk across. Bridge in semi-darkness. Stops to admire the view of the Danube. Hears angry loud swearing in English from below, on the river-bank promenade. Looks down and sees two of the yobs from the restaurant trying to pull the third, who seems unconscious, from out of the river. With some difficulty.
Paul hesitates, then shouts down:

                    PAUL
         Need any help?

                    YOB 1 (ALAN)
                Yeah mate. Gizza-hand.

*Paul runs down to the bank and together they all pull the third yob
(DAVEY) out of the river, dripping wet and barely conscious.
All three have obviously been beaten up. They leave Davey on the
ground and collapse onto a bench by the bank, getting their breath
back. The yobs have solid Liverpudlian accents.*

                    PAUL
                Did the Russians do this?

                    YOB 2 (MIKE) *(startled)*
                Eh? How'd yew know?!

                    PAUL
                I was at the restaurant. You ruined my bloody
                dinner, y'know.

                    ALAN
                Big deal. Nor egg-zaktly fun fer us eider.

                    MIKE
                Yeh, it was the fuckin' Ruskies. Followed us
                and done us over. Bastards.

                    PAUL
                *(recognising the Liverpudlian accents, and slipping back into
                his own)* You're all from Liverpool, aren't yers?
                So why de hell were youse shouting fer *Chelsea*?!!

                    ALAN
                What's it to you mate?

                    PAUL
                I'm Liverpool too, y'know. Well, originally.
                And *nobody* from Liverpool supports Chelsea.
                So what's yer game?

MIKE
So *which* are yer?

PAUL *(gets the point quickly)*
Everton. Evertonian. Name's Paul.

MIKE
Good job. So are we. I'm Mike. He's Alan.
Dat one's Davey. When he's awake.

ALAN
It's our summer job, mate. Better dan the Social
Screw anyway. We gets paid to get pissed and smash
a few places up. Well, we'd do it anyway.
For free, like. But we aint gonna be shouting
'Everton! ' while we does it, now is we. Wouldn't be
right. Let the Chelsea fuckers take the blame.

PAUL
But why here? How come Budapest?

MIKE
Prague last year. We just got moved on, like.

ALAN
We're mercenaries, see, dat's what. Not local.
So we can just disappear.

PAUL
Mercenaries? So who's paying you?

ALAN
'Ave two guesses, right—

MIKE *(interrupts)*
Shurrup Alan. We just gets phone calls. Dunno
who. Davey knew who dey were. Never told us.

ALAN
Gotta right problem, if Davey's had it.
Wake up, soddit—hows we gonna get paid now?

He aims a soft kick at the recumbent Davey—friendly rather than vicious.

MIKE
An' after this lot, I ain't hangin' round to find out. I'm outa-here *tomorra*.

ALAN
No way. I'm gonna get them Ruskies back first. An' I wanna be paid. *(Another friendly kick. Davey just groans)*. Wakey-wakey, pal.

PAUL
Look, lads, I'm off. *He* needs a *hospital*. And I wouldn't take on those Russians if I were you.

ALAN
Turf war. We're up fer it. An' there's a lot bigger fish frying. I wanna be in on it.

PAUL
Look, I'm knackered. Haven't eaten all sodding day, thanks to you lot. Go easy. Get him to a hospital.

MIKE
See ya.

Paul leaves. Alan kicks Davey again casually. Mike nurses his arm.

15. INT. PAUL'S HOTEL ROOM.

PAUL *(on phone)*
Room service? *(pause)* Oh, I see. *(pause)* So what time will breakfast be?

16. EXTERIOR. GELLERT HOTEL POOL. MORNING. BRIGHT SUN.

Written:] MONDAY

Paul is looking for a seat by the fairly crowded side of the Gellert exterior bathing pool, the one with the famous wave machine on the hour. Waiters are serving drinks.

>PAUL *(to passing waiter)*
>Excuse me, can I please get some breakfast here?
>The dining room seemed to be closed.
>
>WAITER
>It is too late for the buffet breakfast, sir.
>And I can only bring you drinks at the pool.
>
>PAUL *(looks at his watch)*

Oh.

Paul suddenly spots the girl from the train, in a fetching swimsuit, just getting out of the pool. She goes to two empty loungers, with towels, nearby. She puts on sunglasses.

>PAUL *(delighted)*
>In that case, a coffee, please. Black.
>Very strong. Er, Room 403. And I'll be over there.
>*(points to the two loungers)*

Paul goes and stands next to the woman as she settles down into one of the loungers.

>PAUL
>Olah, what a lovely surprise! It's good to see you again. May I join you?

A very large stocky middle-aged man—FEKETE—has also pulled himself out of the pool and is now standing nearby, listening.

> WOMAN *(speaks in Hungarian)*
> Tessék. Ismerlek? *(I'm sorry. Do I know you?)*

> PAUL
> I wanted to thank you for your help yesterday.

> WOMAN *(in Hungarian)*
> Én nem értelek. Beszélsz magyarul?
> *(I don't understand you. Do you speak Hungarian?)*

> PAUL *(puzzled)*
> Er, on the train, Olah. We met yesterday.

Fekete intervenes. Very suspicious.

> FEKETE *(in fairly good English)*
> My wife does not speak English, sir.

> PAUL *(baffled, embarrassed)*
> I'm terribly sorry. Your wife? Er, I met Olah yesterday and she was very helpful to me—

> FEKETE
> I see. *(to woman, in Hungarian: Do you know this man?)*
> Tudja, hogy ez az ember?

> WOMAN *(shrugs)*
> Soha nem láttam *(Never seen him before.)*

She gets up and slips back into the pool.

> FEKETE
> My wife does not know you, sir, she says.
> Why are you bothering my wife?

Waiter appears with Paul's coffee on an elaborate tray. Paul distractedly signs the chit for it but is now awkwardly left with nowhere to put the coffee tray down.

PAUL
I'm very sorry, sir. I must have made a dreadful
mistake. I will leave you in peace.

FEKETE *(menacingly)*
No, you do *not* go, sir. I wish to know how you
know my wife's name. Sit, sir.

*Paul hesitates, then sits down on a lounger while Fekete takes the
other, looking very hostile. Paul tries to sip the extremely hot coffee.*

PAUL *(pretty lamely)*
I'm very sorry. It must have been someone else.
Who looks like your wife. With the same name.
Er. You are Mr Olah, yes?

FEKETE
No, sir. My name is Fekete Ervin. My wife's name
was Olah Velma. Now she is Feketene Ervin.

PAUL *(not following)*
I'm terriby sorry if I've made a mistake, Mr Ervin.

FEKETE *(irritated)*
Mr Fekete. *Not* Mr Ervin.

PAUL
I'm sorry, Mr er—?

FEKETE
*(solemnly and pedantically explains, but with a grim
threatening edge to his tone:)*
Fekete is my family name. Ervin is my given name.
I think you misunderstand. In Hungary, when a
woman marries she may change her name.
When, for example, Szendrey Júlia marries Petőfi
Sándor, she may keep her birth name Szendrey
Júlia. Or she may add -né to her husband's full
name, and is called Petőfi Sándorné. Or she may

add -né to her husband's family name, add her own full name and be called Petőfiné Szendrey Júlia. Or she may simply add the -né to her husband's full name, add her own full name and be called Petőfi Sándorné Szendrey Júlia. Do you understand? But none of this, sir, explains how you know my wife's previous name—

A mobile phone rings from under the towel Paul is sitting on.

    FEKETE
(reaches through Paul for the phone) Excuse me, sir.

    PAUL
No, please excuse *me*, Mr Fekete. I have to go. *(tries to dink his coffee quickly—it is too hot)*

    FEKETE *(sharply)*
You will wait, sir. I still wish to know how you know my wife's name if she does not know you. *(then speaks into the phone).* Yes, I speak English. Who? *(longish pause)* How did you get this number? *(pause)* He should not have given it to you. *(longish pause)* I understand. Yes. As arranged. *(pause)* One will be enough. *(pause)* Yes. Yes. You can pick it up in *(looks at his watch)* 30 minutes —at 11.30 sharp. But you should not need to use it. Just wave it about. But be there. On time. Then wait for a call. That is most important. That is all. *(exits phone)* Now, sir—

    PAUL
(who has been trying to leave but has been angrily waved back by Fekete, has now registered the reference to 11.30, is startled, and has looked at his own watch. Quickly:)
Look, Mr Fekete, I *really* must go. I hadn't realised it was that late—I forgot to change the time on my watch last night. And I'm going to be *very* late for something. Some other time, yes. Look— you'll miss the famous wave machine—

As the wave machine in the pool starts and distracts Fekete, Paul gulps down some hot coffee and dashes off.

17. INT. PETŐFI MUSEUM. EXHIBITION ROOMS

Anna is showing Paul the exhibition spaces. They are in the Sandor Petőfi rooms.

PAUL
I'm so sorry I was late. I slept like a log. And I had forgotten to change the time on my watch.

ANNA
Do not worry. We can do the full tour after your talk. But you have probably not heard of any of our writers anyway. People know about Vienna's famous writers and thinkers—Musil, Kraus, Wittgenstein, Freud, of course —but nobody has heard of ours. Even Petőfi Sandor himself.

PAUL
(suddenly remembering Fekete's pedantic explanation)
Er, he was married to Szendrey Júlia, wasn't he?

ANNA
I am *most* impressed! Yes, it is a great romantic tale.
(as she leads him through the sequence of glorious rooms, with mirrors and drapes, she recites, in Hungarian, the third stanza of 'At the End of September')
—Ha eldobod egykor az özvegyi fátyolt,
Fejfámra sötét lobogóul akaszd,
Én feljövök érte a síri világból
Az éj közepén, s oda leviszem azt,
Letörleni véle könyűimet érted,
Ki könnyeden elfeledéd hivedet,
S e szív sebeit bekötözni, ki téged
Még akkor is, ott is, örökre szeret!

— It's a haunting vision of his fear that after his
death Julia will throw away her widow's veil
and not be faithful to his own eternal love for her.
And Julia did in fact re-marry, in 1850, less than a
year after Petőfi's death—or disappearance.
I do not think she wished to be a national icon.
We have her widow's veil on show, over there.

        PAUL
Can you, er, give me any of his poems in English?

        ANNA
Of course. One I like very much, even in English,
is: The sea is rising,
        the sea of the people;
        challenging earth and heaven,
        its dreadful might
        rears up wild waves'—
—And here's where you will be giving your talk.

They enter a splendid large room, with mirrored walls.
And a large TV projection screen.

        ANNA
I understand you want to show some visuals.
So I will hand you over to Josef, our technician.
You can show him what you want, and he will set it
up for you. Then you can leave all your materials
with him, and come and have some lunch.
I will show you our 1956 exhibition on the way.

Paul exchanges greetings with Josef, who does not speak much English.
Paul hands over his laptop and a DVD and starts to show what he
wants by demonstrating on the laptop.

18. EXT. UPON A BRIDGE.

Alan unwraps a small parcel. Inside is a gun, a note, and a brand new
mobile phone. He reads the note, screws it up, takes his old mobile
phone out of his pocket and drops it and the note into the river.

19. INT. DINING ROOM IN THE PETŐFI MUSEUM.

*Gábor and Andrew are waiting. Gábor is on a mobile phone.
One or two staff from the Museum are chatting in the background.*

> GÁBOR *(comes off his mobile phone)*
> Andrew, good news from Georgy. The restaurant is back to normal. His staff have returned. He says he *did* get a phone call this morning—but it was from the Russians!— and *they* have offered him their own 'protection'. "Every body needs a roof over their heads," he said. It's a Russian Mafia saying, apparently. I'm afraid he has, as you say, 'done a deal' —but he has invited us all there for an early dinner this evening, as his guests, before the concert tonight. Would you be happy with that?

> ANDREW
> Well, let's hope it's for the best.

Paul and Anna enter.

> ANDREW
> Ah Paul. Hope you slept well, and saw a bit of Budapest this morning. You're all set up, yes. Right, lunch, then your talk. Then you've got the afternoon free. But there's an open air concert early this evening, 7 p.m. Outside St. Stephen's Basilica. We're the guests of the Museum. And dinner beforehand. Is all that OK for you?

> PAUL
> Absolutely. I'm in your hands. Only hope I can justify it.

MIKE GORMAN enters boisterously, a little late and apologetic. Large man, friendly, ebullient, enthusiastic, impulsive, in his 70s but still robust. (Mike Gambon type)

GORMAN
Hello all. Sorry. Running late.
(greets warmly:) Gábor. Anna.
(less warmly:) Andrew.
And you must be Paul? Good to meet you.
I'm Mike, Mike Gorman. Am I too late for nosh?

ANNA
You're fine, Mike. We were just about to start.
A good Hungarian selection for you: *(gestures at a buffet, full of delicious food. Paul looks hungrier than ever.)* Chicken paprika, stuffed cabbage, kolbasz and csaba sausage, roast duck, roast suckling pig, letcho— that's green peppers, tomatoes and onions, Paul — pasta with fried cabbage, and pasta with curd cheese and bacon. Do take your pick. Paul, you first.

In the short buffet queue Gorman ends up next to Paul.
As they help themselves, with Paul piling up food on his plate hungrily, Gorman talks enthusiastically:

GORMAN
Gather you're talking about John Berger's *Painter of Our Time*, yes? I knew Berger once, way back.
And I knew the guy he modelled his painter, Lavin, on, y'know. In London. Long time ago.

PAUL
You mean Peter Peri?

GORMAN
Well, Peri was one main model of course.
But there was another artist too, Rákos Béla
—a sculptor, though, not a painter.
You should meet him. I'll give you his address.

PAUL
He's still alive? He's in Budapest?

GORMAN
No, no. Lives at Salfod.

PAUL
Salford? Near Manchester?

GORMAN
Good God, no. Sal-*Fod*. Near Balaton, the lake—
Only an hour or so away from here.
Go out and see him. Tell him I sent you.

Josef the technician appears and talks quietly to Anna.

PAUL *(a bit overwhelmed)*
Hang on. I've only got a couple of days.
And I didn't even know about him. But I'm
certainly interested. You must tell me more—

Paul and Gorman take their food to the table to sit.
Paul is just about to take his very first bite. Anna comes over.

ANNA
Paul, I'm terribly sorry, but there seems to be a
problem. Josef can't get your laptop DVD player
to work properly with our projection screen.
Could you possibly come and help him?

PAUL
(Paul looks at the food he was just about to eat —his first
proper bite since arriving. Very reluctantly, he pushes his
plate away.) Of course. I'll be back shortly—I hope.

20. EXT. RESTAURANT. PAVEMENT AREA.

Georgy greets various customers and shows them to tables.
Among them, the distinguished figure of EMRIC LAKATOS
is shown to his favourite table, with another customer friend.

21. INT. PETŐFI DINING ROOM.

The food has mostly gone. Paul enters hurriedly. Goes over to Anna.

        PAUL
I have a rather odd request, Anna. Could I possibly have a length of un-cooked sausage—

        ANNA *(baffled)*
Of course, Paul. I am sure we can find some. You want to eat some sausage?

        PAUL
Not exactly. Er, and a cutting board?

22. EXT. RESTAURANT. PAVEMENT AREA.

A Russian—DIMITRI—arrives and seats himself near the outside enclosure fence and consults the menu. He then makes a call on a mobile phone.

23. INT. LECTURE ROOM IN PETŐFI.

        ANNA *(introducing Paul)*
Welcome to you all, for this lunchtime lecture in our series this year, commemorating the 1956 Budapest uprising. I am sorry that we are running a little late. So, I'll be as brief as possible. Let me introduce Dr. Paul Connor, from England, who is going to give today's British Council sponsored lecture. We are particularly grateful to him since he has had to miss his lunch in order to try to sort out some technical problems. But he seems to have brought some lunch with him! *(to audience laughter, points to sausage and cutting board)* So, without further ado, let me hand over to Dr Paul Connor, who will talk to you about John Berger's novel *A Painter of Our Time* and its relation to the 1956 uprising.

Applause from a fairly full audience.

> PAUL
> Thank you, Professor Kelemen, for that warm introduction. I am very honoured to be here.
> *(picks up a long Hungarian sausage from the cutting board)*
> I'll explain the sausage later—Keeps you guessing. Nothing like suspense. *(mild laughter).*
> This is a talk about time. Our time. So I'd better begin. Simply. Every good story, so they say, has a beginning, a middle, and an end.
> But, as any good story teller will tell you, not — necessarily— in that order.
> *(The audience are mildly on his side.)*
> And a story is not always a kind of straight line going from A through B to C, like a train passing through stations. And neither, perhaps, is time itself.
> If only because: two or more things can happen, as we say, 'at the same time'.
> Indeed, history can be thought of as the many things that happen to happen at the same time. And by doing so, lock those events into place, or into *that* time. *This* happened *then*.
> The events in Hungary in late October 1956 coincided—as we say—with the invasion of Suez, the Franco-Israeli-British invasion of Egypt.
> But did one just *happen* to happen 'at the same time' or did one help to make the other happen, at least in the way that it happened?
> Is history always a kind of collision course?

24. EXT. RADAY STREET.

Shot of Alan walking down Raday Street towards the restaurant, with a bulge in his waistband where he clearly has the gun.
He answers a mobile phone call.

25. INT. LECTURE ROOM IN PETŐFI.

> PAUL *(continuing, but not continuous)*
> Take a different moment. The events in Paris, *les évènements*, in May 1968, and the events in Prague that led to the Soviet intervention in August 1968. Were they just more or less co-incidents?
> Or 1989, when the beginnings of the end of the Berlin Wall, as Hungary opened its borders with Austria, were matched in date with happenings in China that led to the events in Tiananmen Square.
> Did the one in some part happen *because* of the other? Even *reciprocally* in some way. It's when episodes *co-incide* that history seems to move much faster, into what we call a crisis. A memorable moment. A year to remember. 1956. 1968. 1989.
> Two sequences converging into a collision.
> What the film-makers used to call parallel editing.

26. EXT. RADAY STREET.

Shot of two Russians—BORIS, IVAN—walking the other way down Raday street towards the restaurant.

27. INT. PETŐFI LECTURE ROOM

> PAUL
> *(continuing the lecture, but not continuous with previous)*
> John Berger has an image for this speed-up of time. If I want to draw lots of little diamonds, like this:
> *(he does so on the projection screen:* <> <> <> <>*)*
> —it takes a lot of time.
> And each is independent of the others.

28. EXT. RESTAURANT. PAVEMENT AREA.

Boris and Ivan reach the restaurant and sit at a table within the fairly busy pavement seating area.

29. INT. PETŐFI LECTURE ROOM

          PAUL *(continuing the lecture)*
          But what if I now draw one set of lines this way—
          (draws first set of parallel lines at an angle)
          —And then another set of lines *across* the first.
          (he draws a second set at right angles to and crossing the first)
          —eh, *voilà*, immediately *lots* of little diamonds—
          in almost no time at all. Time speeds up at a stroke.
          Or two.

30. EXT. RESTAURANT. PAVEMENT AREA.

Very fast and very smooth sequence:

—*Alan enters the restaurant seating area, pulls out a gun and waves it in the air.*
—*Georgy and customers try to take shelter behind tables.*
—*Boris stands up, pulls a gun, points it at Alan, but without firing.*
—*Alan sees Boris and fires his automatic gun at Boris*
—*Boris then fires back.*
—*Ivan also fires a gun at Alan. Flurry of several gunshots.*
—*Customers panic and scramble to leave.*
—*Alan falls dead, as do two customers at a nearby table.*
— *the dead are Lakatos and his companion.*
—*In the panic rush of customers, in an almost unseen move, Dimitri swiftly picks up Alan's fallen gun and pockets it, while placing another gun near the dead Alan's hand.*
—*Dimitri slips away with the rest of the panicking customers.*
—*Boris and Ivan remain.*

31. INT. PETŐFI LECTURE ROOM.

          PAUL *(continuing the lecture, but* not *continuous)*
          At this point in the novel, one more main character emerges: Lazslo, once a poet and a one-time comrade of Lavin, in political exile after the 1919 attempted revolution in Hungary. We learn through

Lavin's comments in his diary that Lazslo spent the 1940s in Moscow, and returned to Hungary with the Red Army, to become a leading politician in post-war Budapest. But what is the truth about Lazlo—
is he a Soviet collaborator or a Hungarian hero? Revolutionary or opportunist?

32. EXT. RESTAURANT. PAVEMENT AREA.

Armed police have arrived rapidly.
They point their guns at Boris and Ivan, who immediately surrender.
Georgy emerges from hiding behind upturned tables.

33. INT. PETŐFI LECTURE ROOM.

               PAUL *(continuing the lecture, but* not *continuous)*
Talking about one of his major works,
Lavin at one point writes in his diary:
'I was painting *The Waves* while Laszlo was being interrogated.' Note that '*while*'.
Are these two lines of time simply like parallel lines, just happening 'at the same time'?
Note that he is painting a work called *The Waves*.
We speak of time as flowing, and of history as coming in waves, wave after wave.
A wave of protest, a wave of revolutions.
And History can drown us.
Another diary entry reads, in more general terms, as if it's something that happens regularly or often:
' The painter paints still lives *while* men are being shot in the streets.'
So, we sometimes think of our *own* lives
as a kind of time-line, which then *intersects* with some much larger line we call History.
Like this: *(he draws on the projector screen)*

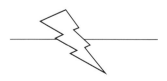

But history is also *other* peoples lives. And deaths.
All the time.

34. EXT. RESTAURANT. PAVEMENT AREA.

It is now a busy police crime scene. Three corpses. Police taking statements from frightened customers, but in the bustle and noise no specific dialogue intelligibly audible. Boris and Ivan are in custody. Ambulances arrive.

35. INT. PETŐFI LECTURE ROOM.

PAUL *(continuing the lecture, but not continuous)*
So you could think of it as the classic flashback technique or detective story device: someone has disappeared, and the detective, John, will back-track and try and find out what really happened. Was it murder? Suicide? A crime? A flight? Except that John is not a detective, but an art critic. Though we do in fact learn, through John's own investigations, that Lavin had indeed left, to return to Hungary. In that significant month, October 1956, the month of the uprising. But *why* he returned is less clear.

36. EXT. RESTAURANT. PAVEMENT AREA.

STEFAN MESZAROS, a senior detective, arrives and carefully picks up the gun near dead Alan's hand. Georgy is identifying Alan as a yob from the previous evening.

37. INT. PETŐFI LECTURE ROOM

PAUL *(continuing the lecture, but not continuous)*
After he hears of Laszlo's execution, Lavin notes in his diary: '*There never was a chance of meeting you again.*'

Think about the time-lines involved in those curious
tenses. But then, quite unexpectedly,
Laszlo is declared to have been innocent after all.
A strange surprise—

A mobile phone rings loudly in the audience.—It is Gábor's mobile phone. He is deeply embarrassed, and the audience laughs.

GÁBOR
I am *so* so sorry Paul.

But Gábor has automatically listened to the voice on the phone. In shock, he gets up and starts to leave the hall. Stumbles out. Camera follows him out, to:

38. INT. JUST OUTSIDE LECTURE-ROOM.

GÁBOR *(In Hungarian, on phone:)*
Igen... Persze... Mi lesz.... Itt? Igen.
(Yes. Of course. We will. Here? Yes.)

39. EXT. RESTAURANT. PAVEMENT AREA.

Georgy hands his phone to Stefan. Brief word from Stefan : 'Tizenöt perc' —In fifteen minutes.

40. INT. PETŐFI LECTURE ROOM.

PAUL *(continuing the lecture, but* not *continuous)*
So, it's time to come clean. About the sausage!
(holds it up, to laughter)
I was hoping simply to show you an excerpt
from a film scripted by Berger, in which he uses
an enormous sausage as a kind of image of history.
But, as I now realise, despite the best efforts of your
technician here, *there was never going to be a chance of that.*
We think we can get the *images* up on the screen
but we can't get any sound track audible.
So: *I* shall provide a version of the dialogue.

And just in case we don't even get the images,
I'll even try to do the whole scene, using this sausage!
A small piece of surreal theatre: me and my sausage!
Here's the scene, anyway, I desperately hope —
note that it's a lecture within a lecture, from Berger's
film directed by Alain Tanner: *Jonah who will be 25 in the
year 2000*—a title about time, of course.
OK, let's try —fingers crossed.

*He starts the computer DVD—the film excerpt comes up on the
projector screen, but with no sound, so the large screen behind him
shows a silent sequence from the Berger & Tanner film, from scene 9
onwards:*

*Colour film. Classroom. The students, boys and girls, are around
seventeen years old. The principal of the high school introduces Marco,
the new history teacher. (The film dialogue is all in French, but no
soundtrack is audible.)*

        PAUL *(commenting)*
The principal introduces the new history teacher,
Marco.

*On screen: The principal leaves the room. Marco, who has been holding
a suitcase, puts it down on the desk and opens it. He takes out a long
piece of sausage, a small block, a cleaver and a metronome, all of which
he shows to the amused and surprised students.*

                    PAUL
            Marco says: Never forget that my father is a butcher
            and my mother sings light opera very well.

On projector screen: Class seen laughing. Marco lays the sausage on the cutting block and flourishes the cleaver, then sets the metronome going.

Paul lays his own sausage on his cutting board.

                    PAUL
            Marco says: Would someone like to come
            and cut the sausage?
            In time with the metronome—

On screen: A boy rushes forward and begins to cut the sausage. Inaudible screams and laughter from the class.

Paul, after an un-responded invitation gesture to his own amused audience, cuts his sausage himself into a few small pieces and one longer one—but his sausage is nowhere near as long as Marco's on the projector screen.

On screen: The boy stops. Marco picks up a few pieces of the cut sausage.

                    PAUL *(flourishing his sausage)*
            Marco says, roughly:
            So these are the pieces, the segments, of history.
            What should we call them?
            Hours? Decades? Centuries? It's all the same and it
            never stops—so is time a sausage?
            Darwin thought so, even though the stuffing
            changed from one end of the sausage to the other.
            Marx thought that some day everyone would stop
            eating sausage. Einstein and Max Planck tore the
            skin off the sausage, which from then on it lost its
            shape.

Paul pauses while an on-screen exchange (in French) is inaudible:

[MARCO: What is sausage skin made of?
A GIRL : Pig's intestine.
MARCO: Very good.]

Paul has now got a copy of the screenplay open in front of him and more or less reads from it while checking the large screen.

        PAUL *(matching Marco on screen)*
Marco says: look at the sausage that's not been cut up yet—You can see its creases, its folds—
What are time's folds made of? —
Marco then gives a short account of history:

In agricultural societies, men believed that time consisted simply of cycles, of seasons.
Each winter solstice contained the same moment.
An individual grew old—but that was simply because he wore himself out: he was the fuel which made the machine of the seasons go. *(pauses)*

Capitalism will supply the idea of time-as-highway. The Highway of — 'Progress'. The idea that the conquerers hadn't simply won a battle, but that they had been chosen—because they were superior beings —Their superiority would span the cycles and the seasons. It transformed them into corkscrews—of which they were the tip.
And with that tip they opened the bottles of the lesser cultures, one after the other.
They drank—and tossed aside the bottles—
This was a new kind of violence.

In the past, the arrow or the sword had killed.
But what killed now was the verdict of history itself. The history of the conquerors—But with this new violence arose a new fear among the conquerors— a fear of the past, a fear of the lesser beings in their broken bottles.—Since if the past could one day overtake the conquerors, it would show

as little pity as they had shown—
During the nineteenth century, this fear of the past
was transformed—into scientific law.
Time became a road without curves. The length of
the road was now a terrifying abstraction,
but it is not abstractions which take revenge.
From that point on, the thinkers of the nineteenth
century opted for the fear of thought, while
eliminating the fear of the savage and his arrows.
And their roads had boundaries.
Absolutely regular intervals. Millions of years
divided into eras, into dates, into days and into
hours of work to punch in on the time-clock.
Like a sausage cut into segments. *(pauses)*

Now, let me skip forward a bit,
with apologies to Berger and Tanner's film.

On screen: The image fast-forwards at twice the normal playing speed:

Cut to Max's apartment. Morning. Max gets up, sits on the edge of his bed and leafs through the newspaper as he's waking. There are newspapers everywhere. He puts down his paper and goes over to a bureau to take out a piece of clothing. He opens a drawer.

Screen film changes from colour to black & white. Close-up of drawer & revolver; pan left-right following Max; frame in close medium shot.

Inside the drawer is a revolver. Max takes it and aims at his reflection in a mirror. On the bureau is an alarm clock. Max aims at it and fires. The clock flies to pieces.

End of Black & White.

On screen, back to normal speed and to colour:
Marco is speaking in the classroom.

         PAUL *(continues, matching Marco)*
Marco continues, roughly:
today the highway of capitalism is collapsing—

In an acorn are already present the creases which
will give the oak its shape. What you are,
each one of you, was already present at the moment
of your conception— in your first cell there was a
message which you are now in the process of
reading. There are things which make holes in time.
And the holes line up perfectly

On screen: Marco draws a diagram on the blackboard:

PAUL

Marco explains the holes that line up in or as
history, which loops upon itself, neither simply
linear nor cyclical. He says: —you can run a spit
right through the holes in history—
Time bends so that the holes can coincide—
but even prophets only get halfway through the
holes—They exist between times—
No one understood much about Diderot until
an entire generation screamed 'Monster' at Freud—
so much time was needed to pass through the hole.
The holes which prophets make for looking into the
future are the same through which historians later
peer at the stuff of the past. Look at them peering
through the holes dug by Jean-Jacques Rousseau in
order to explain the eighteenth century to us.

Paul pauses the DVD. The image freezes.

>PAUL
>The scene ends with Marco leading the class in an ever increasing beat, a rhythm belted out on their desktops. Time is the opposition between each beat, and as the beat speeds up, time is sliced ever smaller.
>As the past catches up. Speeds up. Towards crisis. Towards moments that shift the tempo of history. As in 1956. 1968. 1989. Those holes which line up in history. And those holes are partly composed of the absences, the gaps, the felt needs which are *not* met, the demands which are passed on from one crisis to another, like the holes created by electrons as they ricochet down a wire carrying what we call an electric current. — But these are *my* comments, not something Marco says. Let me just run the sequence.

On screen: silent, still no soundtrack: Marco beats on his desk and the students take up his lead. Inaudible laughter and screams. Marco is shouting something. The rhythm of the drumming intensifies. The whole class bangs on their desks. Marco yells something. He whistles with his fingers. Students imitate him. Drumming continues growing faster, the class goes wild. Screams and laughter. Marco howls something. (All this in complete silence on the projector screen.)

>PAUL
>Marco yells: With total synthesis, time disappears! *(pauses)* Now, what do we make of this extraordinary sequence?

Paul stops the DVD player. Cut to:

41. INT. HALL OUTSIDE LECTURE ROOM.

Gábor is writing a note. Takes a moment or two.
He enters at back of lecture room and waits for the lecture to finish.

42. INT. PETŐFI LECTURE ROOM.

    PAUL *(continuing the lecture, but not continuous)*
So John Berger is constantly trying to *image*
how time loops, freezes, slows, speeds up,
how history is *not* continuous, and so is open to
revolution, not closed and simply linear,
not uniform and predictable,
but composed of crises, of change.

In a later work, *Another Way of Telling*,
he again uses the image of a line,
this time to think about photographs.
Here's one of the photos he used.
It was taken by André Kertesz, the Hungarian
photographer. I think you'll recognise it.

Brings up photo on screen. The photo fills the entire cinema screen.
Pause.

Hold on the photograph.
Then cut back to Paul speaking with the image behind him.

    PAUL
We can think of this as a moment cut out of time,
as if time were a line and taking the the photo cuts
across it, freezes it. Like this. *(Writes on display.)*

--------------------[/]---------------------

But, suggests Berger, what if we think of the photo
more as a kind of cross-section of a moment—
a convergence of possible lines,
which then makes the rest of the line *provisional, even
though* it actually happened:
(he redraws the diagram)

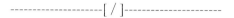

The photo, if you like, turns time towards us,
turns it into a circle, facing us, full of possibilities,
echoes, connections, open futures.
A photo can be the cross-hairs of history.

What if we tried to entitle this photo,
as one might a painting.
What should we call it? Look at the faces.
Parting? The Accusation? *(pauses)*

In fact, Keretsz entitled it:
' A Red Hussar Leaving, June 1919 '.
Say we gloss that title a little—
' Leaving to fight for socialism, 1919'.
The photo, especially with that title,
captures different times in one space.
A past, and several futures, and several non-futures.
We think we know 'what happened' in 1919.
The Budapest Soviet.
And we *do* know what did *not* happen. It was defeated.

But we do *not* know what *might* have happened,
which is what this image reveals to us,
through a hole in history: the intentions of these
people were part of what *might* happen, and therefore
part of the reason why what happened *did* happen.

How we are able, now, to describe the events of
'1919' is not the same as how the people in this photo
would have described what they thought, hoped,
imagined, and feared might be about to happen.
History is not pre-determined in advance and what
happens is only made sense of, in many circumstances,
such as a revolution, or an uprising, by what people
thought was going to happen, and *could* happen,
and what they judged *should* happen.
History is not only what did happen.
As the photo shows us.

But how, then, do we—those who come after—
judge what *did* happen? Remember that it is part of
that moment that some people, even if they knew
in advance that they *would be defeated*, would *still*
choose as they did. That is one reason why fiction,
its imagined pasts and futures,
remains so crucial in our understanding of what *did*
happen, what we now call history.
What we remember as what happened, once.
What we forget did not happen.

As Paul is finally finishing the lecture, Gábor has walked quietly to the front of the seating to give a note to Anna. She reads it. In shock.

       PAUL
So, finally, may I end on a personal note—
of two memories, overlaid upon each other.
For I have a clear memory of somebody else's
memory: of my father telling me how,
at the age of 12, in 1956, he listened
to the very last broadcast from Budapest Radio,
as the Soviet tanks rolled in.
It said: 'Do not forget us. Do not forget us'.
He told me he would never forget that plea.
Which explains my choice of this topic today.
'Do not forget us.'
We don't. We won't. I'll end there.

ANNA

Thank you so much, Paul, for a memorable lecture. *(pauses)* I could not but think of my own father in 1956, also aged 12, fighting in the Children's Brigade at the Corvin Cinema. And I was so looking forward to our discussion— *(longish pause)* But: I am very sorry that I have to announce some absolutely terrible news. And unfortunately we will have to cut this occasion short. *(pause)* The police are arriving in a few moments, and they need to interview some of us, including perhaps even Dr Connor. *(audience alarm)* But no, it is not like the old days—this concerns a dreadful shooting that has just taken place and they think some of us may be able to offer useful information. But the truly terrible news is that among the bystanders accidentally shot seems to be Professor Emric Lakatos, whom many of you know.
(there is widespread consternation in audience) So, now, with all our apologies, may I ask you please simply to show your appreciation for Dr Connor's talk—

Audience applauds briefly but breaks up in considerable confusion.

Gábor comes over to Paul, Anna and Andrew at the front.

GÁBOR

Paul, I am so so sorry. I must explain. There has been another—incident at Georgy's restaurant. One of those English hooligans came back with a gun and fired at two of the Russians. One of the Russians shot him. But others were also killed in the cross-fire. Tragically, these included Emric Lakatos. Since the dead hooligan was one of those at Georgy's last night, the police want to know if we can tell them anything about what happened last night. But I really do not think we should involve Paul in this. It is clearly a feud between different criminal gangs. Andrew, what do you think?

Paul is distracted by seeing Lea, in jeans and tee-shirt, at the back of the audience.

> PAUL
> In fact, I think there *is* something I should tell you. And the police. —But could you please just excuse me for a moment. There is somebody I have to see.

To their surprise, Paul goes to the back of the room.

> PAUL *(to Lea)*
> What on earth happened this morning?

> LEA *(pleased to see him, but puzzled by this)*
> I don't understand? What do you mean, what happened?

> PAUL
> But I tried to talk to you.

> LEA
> When?

> PAUL
> This morning. At the Gellert Hotel.

> LEA *(teasing)*
> I think, Mr Paul, that you have been having fantasies—or hallucinations. Do you often imagine having conversations with strange women?

> PAUL
> Maybe. Do you blame me? Look, I'm baffled. Can we meet? Please? For coffee. Whatever.

> LEA
> Well, if you wish. I have breakfast—or whatever — every morning in the Iparművészeti Muzeum, just round the corner from here. I could meet you there tomorrow —around 9.30. And it's the nicest place

in all Budapest to have breakfast. The Museum of Applied Arts—the IMM. Would that suit? Alright? They want you back now—

Paul goes back to Gábor, Anna, Andrew. They have been talking to Mike Gorman.

> PAUL
> I'm very sorry about that. It was sort of important.
>
> GORMAN
> Small world. I didn't know you knew Lea?
>
> PAUL
> I'm not sure I do!
>
> GORMAN *(as he goes off to talk to Lea)*
> 'Scuse me. Be with you in a minute.
>
> PAUL
> Look, there's something I should probably tell the police. I ran into those three thugs again last night, after the meal at Rady Street, and I talked to them, briefly. I *might* be able to help.
>
> ANDREW
> I rather think you should steer clear, Paul. It'll only complicate matters and you're due to leave in thirty-six hours.
>
> GÁBOR
> Yes, Paul, I agree with Andrew. I think you should stay out of this. Mike Gorman has agreed to look after you till we're free of the police. He'll take you to Gerbeauds for coffee and cake— and you really shouldn't miss that .
>
> ANNA
> Don't worry. Paul, we'll mention what you've told us to the police, but I doubt if they will want to

interview you. It's not as if you know anything about the Budapest underworld!

ANDREW
Just relax and enjoy yourself for an hour or two. We'll go see the police and meet you at Gerbeaud's later.

GORMAN *(comes over)*
Right, Paul, let's get you a late lunch at least! No sausages though. Cake, the famous Gerbeaud cakes.

43. EXT. STREET.

As they leave and walk to Gerbeauds.

GORMAN
Interested in what you, or Berger, were saying about photography. Must think more about it.
You're coming to my book launch tomorrow, I hope. I was supposed to be doing a re-issue of my photos from '56 and from '89. Different kinds of revolution, that sort of angle. But it's worked out differently. Liked your point about how two events converge and interact. But then how do you take photographs of convergence, of history, or of 'events' at all?

PAUL
Tell me, Mike, how did you get involved in '56?

GORMAN
I was in Vienna. Seeing Europe for the first time. Eighteen years old! First camera as well. Rank amateur. Been hoping to make a living somehow, so invested every last penny I had in a decent camera.
Caught a lift on an Austrian ambulance when the rising broke out and studied the Leica manual all the way to Budapest. Only just managed to make it work by the time I got here. The *Time* stringer only had one staff photographer with him—so anybody with a decent camera got put to work immediately. I was just lucky.

44. INT. POLICE STATION. STEFAN'S OFFICE.

STEFAN
(Efficient, plodding. Speaks in careful English for Andrew's benefit.) So, you say the Russians followed these hooligans, after they left? We know that one of the British boys was beaten up, since he was left at a hospital early this morning. Unconscious. He's in intensive care. That was presumably the Russians. So did the other thug come back for revenge? To shoot up the restaurant? Or even looking for the Russians? The Russians claim he fired first, and they were only defending themselves. And we have witnesses who support that. *(pause)* A very nasty business. Though the case is clear enough, I think. But we have no ID for either the British thug in the hospital or for the dead one. And, most unfortunately, this little vendetta has had one tragic side-effect. The death of Emric Lakatos. He was in the way of one of the bullets. But it now seems that his murderer, the British boy, is dead himself.

GÁBOR
The death of Emric Lakatos is a real blow to us all.

STEFAN
Did you know him personally?

GÁBOR
Back in '89, yes. Quite well, then.
And I would see him at Georgy's. He has his lunch —*used to* have his lunch— there most days. But he moved in a different world from me now.

ANNA *(hesitantly)*
We don't know any more about these British hooligans, but our visiting lecturer has told us that he met them late last night, by chance. He may be able to tell you more.

ANDREW *(quickly)*
I very much doubt it, Inspector. He's only just
arrived in Hungary. He would hardly have any
information about what looks like a Mafia feud—

STEFAN
A Mafia feud? So, why do you say that? It looked
like a matter of simple hooliganism and revenge.
And the Russians are Embassy staff.
They are claiming diplomatic status.

GÁBOR *(cautiously)*
Well, I cannot be sure, of course, but yesterday
evening may have been a *charade*, a set up job—
to persuade Georgy to take out protection on his
restaurant. Did Georgy tell you this? From the
very Russians who intervened. And we thought
that perhaps the British hooligans were paid by the
Russians to stage the incident —and something
went wrong—perhaps they weren't paid enough, or
asked too much . . .

STEFAN *(pause)*
An interesting hypothesis. Perhaps I should speak to
your guest lecturer, after all. Where can I find him?

GÁBOR
He'll be at Gerbeauds by now.

STEFAN
Mr Bradley, may I please ask you to go with my
officers to identify Mr Connor and to return here
with him. *(waves away Andrew's gesture of protest)*
I am sorry to trouble you, but —

45. EXT. TABLES OUTSIDE GERBEAUDS.

> GORMAN *(reading the menu's delights)*
> Now. Doesn't this make your mouth water? This is what I've ordered for you—A selection of their specialities: *(he reads gloatingly from the menu)* — Diplomat pudding: a scrumptuous Hungarian dessert, named, some say, after Nesselrode, the famous Russian diplomat who was known for his passion for English puddings. Dobos layer cake: máglyarakás—that's layers of biscuits and apples, topped with whipped egg whites. Somlói galuska: a combination of white and chocolate cake and vanilla pudding covered with chocolate sauce and whipped cream. Vargabéles: baked pasta and cottage cheese with raisins. Gundel crêpes—filled with walnuts and topped with chocolate sauce and whipped cream. And various strudels to fill in. — Ah! here it comes.

Just as the waiters arrive with a very large order of assorted cakes, a police car with siren wailing clears a route across the square to come to a stop in front of their table. Andrew and the police officer get out. Just as their cakes are put on the table.

> ANDREW
> Very sorry, Paul. I have to take you to see a police inspector, after all. Now. About last night. Damn nuisance. But don't worry, you're not being arrested.

Customers are intrigued. Paul is embarrassed, and looks very longingly at the cakes as they arrive in quantity.

> GORMAN
> Don't worry about the cake, Paul.
> It won't be wasted. I'll happily eat it for you!

Paul gets into the police car, which exits the square with wailing siren.

46. INT. STEFAN'S OFFICE.

A longish time has lapsed. Andrew is impatient. Paul is very tired. And very hungry. There are just some empty coffee cups on the table.

    STEFAN *(pedantically checking off his notes)*
—So, to summarise, yet again: You say these hooligans told you they were being paid to cause trouble, but you do not know by whom. They did not tell you. In fact *they* did not know, you say. Only the one who is dead knew?
Or the one who was drowning? But it may have been the Russians. And they did this also in Prague. Last year. As 'mercenaries'. But all you can really tell me is their names, their personal names, not even their family names.
So: we are to look for three people called: Mike, Alan, and Davey. Or Michael, Alan, and David. From Liverpool. You are also from Liverpool. But you do not know them? You had not met them before. A blank. *(pause)*
So: we might be able to check hotels and passport control. But they could have come into the country several ways, without having records taken. And they may not even be known at their hotel by those names. *(pause)* But they were in Prague last year. So: there may be a police record, if they caused trouble there. The one in the river that you say is called Davey is still unconscious, and is not in fact likely to recover. And the third one said he was leaving. That is our best bet. Has he left?
An Englishman buying a plane or train ticket at very short notice. We are checking. *(pause)*
So: that is all we have, yes?

    ANDREW *(utterly exasperated)*
Inspector, we have now been over this several times already. Do we really have to stay while you solve the whole crime? We have a concert to get to, which starts in ten minutes.

> STEFAN *(ignores him; to Paul:)*
> And you really do not know what was meant by the phrase 'bigger fish to fry'? A red herring perhaps?

> ANDREW *(emphatically)*
> We are extremely sorry if a national hero has been shot in this unfortunate business, but I really must insist that the British Embassy be informed if we are to be kept here any longer. Dr. Connor is a guest of the British Council after all.

> STEFAN *(very reluctantly)*
> Alright, you may both go. I was hoping that we would receive some further information from our inquiries while you were still here. But, yes, a police car will take you to your concert. That is the best I can now do. But contact me, please, if you do remember anything else, anything at all. Yes?

47. EXT. THE PLAZA OUTSIDE ST. STEPHEN'S BASILICA. A STUNNING SETTING FOR AN OPEN-AIR CONCERT.

The concert is just about to begin, with the Compére already making an announcement in Hungarian (content as in the English below). A wailing siren interrupts him, as a police car arrives at high speed to deposit, very visibly, Paul and Andrew. With considerable disruption, they are then quickly ushered to their seats, nearly at the front, next to Gorman, Gábor and Anna. With enormous embarrassment, Paul settles into his seat, next to Gorman, and tries to lose himself.

> GORMAN *(whispers)*
> Getting quite a reputation for being escorted by police sirens! Even the Ruskies are impressed.

Gorman nods to indicate what is clearly a Russian Embassy group. Paul spots Colonel Voroshensky among them.

PAUL *(whispers)*
Small city, Budapest.

GORMAN
And *everybody* comes to these concerts.

COMPERE
(continuing now in English, irritated)
And for those from elsewhere who are visiting us, or *(pointedly)* have arrived late, let me repeat: that this concert is being dedicated to the memory of Emric Lakatos who, as most of you will by now have heard, was unfortunately killed in a stupid shooting incident this afternoon. So, with great sadness, we dedicate this evening to the memory of a true leader and hero of '89.

As the music begins:

PAUL *(whispers)*
Don't suppose you brought any spare cake with you? I missed dinner. Again. Stuck in the police station.

GORMAN
Sorry.

PAUL
Look, I'm absolutely knackered.
Wake me up when it's all over.

He closes his eyes and sleeps.

Glorious music in glorious setting . . .

Simply enjoy for a few moments. A kind of interval.

48. EXT. CONCERT.

At the end of the concert, Paul is gently woken by Anna. He apologises profusely and with embarrassment for sleeping right through it.

        PAUL
I'm *so* sorry. —But I *was* listening—
I just had my eyes closed.

        GORMAN *(amused)*
And the enthusiastic snoring was an appreciative accompaniment, was it?

        PAUL
I'm sorry. Look, I only came to give a lecture.
I didn't think it would be this exciting!

        ANDREW
It's all right, Paul, you've had a rough day, and I've been neglecting you. I'll drive you straight to the Gellert. We don't want any more adventures, do we. You can get a good night's sleep at least.

        GORMAN
Never mind, Paul, I may have a pleasant surprise for you tomorrow—and Lea tells me you're meeting her for coffee, yes?

        PAUL
I'm not sure I should. Isn't that her over there?

        GORMAN
Where?

Paul points. Among the crowd milling around at the close of the concert, a woman in an expensive plunging neckline evening dress, is making her way to an exit from the concert enclosure, some distance away. Fekete is near her, talking to someone.

                    PAUL
          There. With Fekete, or whatever his name is,
          her husband.

*Paul takes out his mobile phone and takes a surreptitious snap of the
woman. But Fekete sees him take the photo. Highly indignant
reaction. Starts to move angrily through the crowd towards Paul.
But he is then pulled away by someone in the crowd.*

                    GORMAN
          (as they quickly leave by another exit)
          Ah, I see. Well, Paul, don't worry too much about
          Fekete. He's a pretty nasty piece of work.
          But you should be all right to meet Lea..

                    PAUL
          He's a nasty piece of work, you say, and I'm meeting
          his wife for breakfast! Why shouldn't I worry!?

                    GORMAN
          It's a common mistake. But that's Buda.
          (Paul is baffled.) Lea is Pest. I admit, you sometimes
          have to look pretty closely—above the waist.
          But the hilly one is Velma, the flatter one is Lea.
          They're sisters :Velma and Lea. They're well known
          around Budapest. And *Velma* is the one married to
          Fekete's money. Lea is as poor as a dormouse.
          Are you sure you've picked the right one? *(laughs)*

                    PAUL
          I've made a right fool of myself, haven't I. Again.

49. INT . PAUL'S HOTEL ROOM

*Paul takes the uncooked sausage from the lecture out of his briefcase
and looks hungrily at it. Decides against. Looks at the photo of
(Velma-Lea) on his mobile phone.*

PAUL *(to himself)*
If music be the food of love, play on. —
Let's just make sure it's the right dish.

50. INT. COFFEE AREA INSIDE IPARMŰVÉSZETI MUZEUM (THE I.M.M.)

Written:] TUESDAY

Paul and Lea are sitting at one of the little tables, with just coffee and croissants. Paul has brought flowers.
He is looking glumly at his meagre breakfast.

PAUL
You said it was the best place in Budapest
for breakfast—

LEA
I said it was the *nicest* place for breakfast.
I meant the building—Isn't it lovely?

PAUL
Yes. But they only serve coffee and croissants!
I skipped the breakfast at the Gellert for this—
well, also to avoid running into your sister
and her husband again.

LEA *(laughs)*
I'm glad you sorted that out! Velma phoned me
about you mistaking her for me at the Gellert!
Any rate, you now owe her a favour.
You said you wanted to meet the sculptor,
Rákos Béla, in Balaton. Well, it's now possible,
since Velma's going to lend me her car. And Mike
Gorman is going to introduce you to old Béla and
you'll even see a bit of Hungary on the way.
The Lake is beautiful at this time of the year.
So, after Mike's book launch, we'll drive to Balaton,
it's only a couple of hours away, then have a late

lunch with my grandmother, Hugi, visit Béla in the afternoon, and return for the evening here, your last night in Budapest. How does all that suit?

PAUL
Absolutely terrific. That's great. Your grandma lives at the lake? And your parents?

LEA
No, both our parents were killed in the '80s.
We were just tiny. Hugi brought us both up pretty well solo—grandfather died in prison in the '50s, after the rising. But since we've grown up, Velma and I have gone our separate ways.
She wanted safety, security, money, status—so obviously she married a crook.
I just wanted to become an eco-architect.

PAUL
Tell me more about you.

LEA
No, you tell me more about you.

PAUL
OK, a compromise. Tell me about Emric Lakatos. Was he really a hero?

LEA
Lakatos was famous in the '80s as one of the leaders of the campaign against the huge Danube Dam, which would have ruined the river in order to generate hydro-electric power—but I don't know if he was still a hero — he almost seemed to have switched sides in the past few years—he became a government consultant on the pipeline projects.

PAUL
Which are?

                    LEA
Well, there are two competing pipelines which are
planned across Hungary — and they need expert
appraisal, but also political decision — which one to
support, which one to block? One is Russian-
backed, the other favoured by the EU. He was due
to give his recommendation as to which one
Hungary should support, in a report due very soon.
But Lakatos also came out a few years ago in favour
of a hugely controversial plan for an incredibly
stupid road bridge right across Lake Balaton, which
suited the government, but of course his old
comrades regarded him as a traitor to the Green
cause.

                    PAUL
And now what's going to happen to his report?

                    LEA
Nobody knows. Now, no more questions.
Look, Mike's book launch is in half an hour—
but if we leave now I can show you something on
the way that Anna mentioned yesterday.
The flowers are lovely, by the way—thanks,
but is it OK if I leave them here for the next people
at the table—I'm not walking through Budapest
traffic carrying a huge bouquet of flowers!

51. EXT. CAR PARK.

Velma parks her distinctive yellow car in a car park.
Another car has been covertly following her and is now at the entrance.
In the back seat, Dimitri tells the driver to drive in after her and park
nearby. They watch her. She walks away.

52. EXT. OUTSIDE THE CORVIN CINEMA.

Lea and Paul are at the memorial to the children of the Kids Brigade who fought there during the rising. She points out the remaining bullet holes in the walls. The cinema is showing a double bill of Miklós Jancsó, The Red and the White, and István Szabó, Love.

>   LEA
> This is what Anna meant about her father.
> He fought in the kids' brigade during the rising.
>
>   PAUL
> Was he killed?
>
>   LEA
> Her father! How could he have died at 12!
>
>   PAUL
> Sorry. My brain doesn't seem to work when I'm with you. I'm daft.
>
>   LEA *(grins)*
> Do I take that as a compliment, then?

53. INT. ERVIN SZABÓ LIBRARY. A BEAUTIFUL ROOM.

Exhibition panels showing large photos from Gorman's book.
A projector showing a continuous slide show of more photos from the book. Gábor and Anna in the fairly small audience.
Andrew quietens the audience and introduces Gorman.

>   ANDREW
> It gives me great pleasure, on behalf of the Britsh Council, which is sponsoring this exhibition, to welcome you all and to introduce Mike Gorman — to those very few who don't already know him and his work. Mike was here in '56, then had a

renowned career as a war photographer in Biafra and Vietnam, was memorably in Paris in '68, then in Nicaragua. He was in Poland during the rise of Solidarity and in Berlin for the fall of the Wall. But after 1989 he decided to retire, and settled in Budapest, where he is not *entirely* retired. He still takes photos, for the Budapest Preservation Society, and has now helped to photograph every old Budapest building—all 30,000 of them. Mike won the Podmaniczky Medal for helping prevent the thoughtless destruction of such buildings. Part of that work appears in his new book, which we are delighted to be here to celebrate. So, some words, please, Mike. I know words are not your forté but you can't avoid it today.

While Gorman talks, a projection screen lovingly shows photos of old Budapest and then of 1956. They fill the screen. A slow silent sequence with cross-fades.

GORMAN
Thanks Andrew. Morning everybody.
Many thanks for coming. But it's the photos and what they're of, that matters, not me.
So I suggest you really just look at the slide-show, while I ramble on a bit.

I was going to do a book with photos of '56 and of '89, as two different historical moments. But what is a historical moment, after all? And how do you photograph history? So the book has ended up a bit different—it's still "about" 1956, but it begins in 1896 and ends in 2006—about fifty years either side, or, if you prefer, with '56 in the middle. History is change, and that doesn't only happen in crisis moments, but in long waves, slow processes, small gradual shifts. Like houses falling down. Or new streets emerging.
Or people ageing.

So you're getting two books for the price of one.
History and Heritage. One inside the other.
I'd better make it clear that I didn't actually *take* the photos from 1896—I'm not *quite* that old.
But I did find them, and even that's getting a lot harder to do. It's difficult now to find old photos in junk shops. It's difficult even to find proper junk shops. People just don't keep old photos or photo albums any more, and even if they do they always want to scan them into a computer, tidy them up, put them through some digital clean-up operation so they look brand-new —and then they lose or even throw away the originals. Just as people want to put old buildings through the heritage mill. It's not always wise.

Past time isn't frozen, after all. Old photos show us that. The faces of a past period continue to age, like wine, like a phrase of music. Photos themselves age. The patina on an old photo shows the fragility of time. And time is the essence in a photo.

You have to time your shot. A snap decision. That's why they're called snaps—or used to be. These days, with cameras taking a thousand frames a second, there's less craft. I'm suspicious of digital cameras, even more of mobile phone cameras. But maybe I'm just a grumpy old man, whose ancient craft is dying.

Snap. It was a snap decision to get on an ambulance heading for a place I'd never been to before: Budapest, in 1956. I've told the story before. My first Leica, and I spent the trip from Vienna desperately reading the manual. I've brought it with me today. That's the real focus of the history, for me. The camera. For those snap decisions.
(The battered Leica is in front of him.)
It still works. Beautifully.

But even if you're there, you can't photograph a 'historical event'. Only an incident. An anecdote. Not a story. A moment, not the narrative. A flash of light, never an explanation. A snap. A snip.

All the 400 photos in a huge book celebrating four decades of the great Magnum photo-news agency would together have taken a total of only about 4 to 5 seconds to snap. All 400 of them in 400 split seconds. Forty years of news. In four hundred fragments of seconds. Shards of time. Four hundred still moments.

For about ten years I actually lived off the reprints of just a few snaps that I took in a few split seconds in just a few days. There's still a trickle of income from those copyrights, but now there's lots of movie footage of '56, up on the net, on free websites. That's fine, in its way. But would anybody even publish those photos today? Except to show them for just a split second, on the rolling 24-hour news. There. Gone. An instant. Forgotten.

Snap. There's another sense of snap—the game where you spot the same card or object twice and score a point. History repeats itself, once as tragedy, once as farce—first as history, then as heritage. Snap. Got that one.

1956 and 1989 and even 9/11 are now being re-cycled as consumer products. And some of the 1956 historical bullet holes they show you are now fakes, the buildings touched up, like digital photos.

Snap. Things snap too. Revolutions are breaking points, when contradictions bite, when systems and powers collapse—deadly and fraught, unpredictable, like breakdowns, like somebody snapping.
Like an eco-system failing. Breaking point.

Snap. Snap. But you can't *photograph* the *present* contra-dictions—everything you can *see* these days looks clean and above board, tidied up by the public relations and image men, flat, hollow, shiny plastic. Our conflicts now are not battles, dust, and gunfire, but the fight against inflation. Not storming winter palaces, but suffering credit squeezes. Not uprisings, but rising interest rates and energy prices. Not street warfare but, above all, climate change. And it is what we are *not* doing about our changes to our climate that now constitutes our global crisis — and you *cannot photograph* a *lack* of action or a deliberate refusal to act. So has the medium itself lost its edge? Or could we never really photograph history anyway? Only its ghost.

Any rate, that's enough, and no questions please. Just look at the photos—and buy the damn book! Thank you.

Round of applause. Gorman comes over to Lea and Paul, and gives each a copy of his new book.

GORMAN
Right, let's hit the road for Balaton, just as soon as we can. I'm not sure I like these occasions much.

54. EXT. CAR PARK. BEHIND LIBRARY.

Gorman, Lea and Paul walk into the car park.
Paul is carrying the books, Gorman his Leica.

Dimitri, from the back of his parked car, sees them walking towards Velma's yellow car. Signals to his driver.

As Lea unlocks her sister's car, Paul clumsily drops their books: both bend down to pick them up—and bang heads. Again.

Exactly as they do so, Dimitri's car drives past very close and he fires an automatic pistol. Paul pushes Lea onto the ground and dives on top of her, while Gorman instantly aims the Leica and flashes it point-blank into Dimitri's eyes, then rapidly again into the driver's eyes, semi-blinding both, as their car drives off erratically, nearly crashing as it exits the car park.

Paul picks himself off Lea. Paul is slightly wounded.

> GORMAN
> Let's get you to hospital—there's one just nearby.

> PAUL:
> I'm fine. *(he faints.)*

55. INT. A HOSPITAL TREATMENT ROOM.

Paul is sitting, with Gorman, Lea, Gábor, Anna, Andrew, around him. He has a bandage over a slight flesh wound, barely a scratch. Inspector Stefan is there, explaining—

> STEFAN *(ponderously)*
> —We have tracked the car, we think, to the Russian Embassy compound. That is as far as we can take it at present. But are they actually Russian mafia? If so, what are they up to? We've suspected for some time that Fekete has local mafia connections, though we cannot pin it on him. So our main working hypothesis is that it is the Russian Mafia versus the Hungarian Mafia—part of an ongoing turf war over restaurants, credit cards, etc. And now it is also a vendetta—the Russians are attacking Fekete by trying to kill Velma—since there was obviously a mistake—the two sisters were confused because Lea was driving her sister's car—

GORMAN
Well, maybe. But hang on. Here's a different take on it: Paul has twice mistaken Velma for Lea, so Fekete might have thought something had been going on between Paul and Velma. So Fekete hired the hit on his own wife—but then the mistake between the sisters was made by the guys he hired—

PAUL
—Or number three: maybe they were actually after me, not Lea, and not Velma. But why? Or number four: it was somehow another charade, not serious but a staged attack, like the Liverpool yobs putting on their act at the restaurant? To distract from some 'bigger fish'— whatever that is?

LEA
Well, obviously the biggest fish so far is Emric Lakatos—*if* his shooting *wasn't* an accident, a crossfire victim, but a deliberate hit—perhaps because of the pipeline report?

STEFAN *(plodding, but clear)*
I think you are all becoming 'carried away', yes? By simple coincidences. That last suggestion about Emric Lakatos is *highly* unlikely, when you think about it. Anyone who planned to murder Lakatos would not have used amateur English hooligans for the hit. And even if it *was* a deliberate hit, perhaps by the Hungarian mafia, using the hooligans in some way, what is their interest in the pipeline that Lakatos was due to report on? Our local mafia just deal in credit cards, not global petro-chemical wars.

GORMAN
—But did they assume that Lakatos was going to recommend the Russian pipeline and that would bring in the real mafia, the Russian big boys?
Or did the Russian petro-billionaires assume he was going to recommend the EU pipeline instead, and

then they somehow used an apparent Mafia feud to rub him out?

STEFAN
No. No. No. Either way, it was very risky to take the chance, since nobody actually *knew* which way Lakatos was going to decide, and they might have guessed the wrong decision. It would be *very* short-sighted to murder the man who was actually going to recommend *your* pipeline. If, of course, this has anything at all to do with pipelines. But, on any scenario in which the late Emric Lakatos is central, you three are clearly quite irrelevant—except, perhaps, as a detour or a decoy. There was no reason at all for you three to be shot at—*unless* Lea was being mistaken for Velma. Which only takes us back to a jealous husband, or to a local Mafia feud.

GÁBOR
Or neither.

LEA
All of which doesn't answer the immediate question. Paul is fit to travel and we're due at Lake Balaton. So do we have to hang around? Can we please go?

STEFAN
Well, I cannot actually stop you. And I do not think I need to. You have told me all you think you know.

GÁBOR
I think it's actually safest to go to Balaton anyway.

ANDREW
I agree. After all this, Paul, you need to relax—take a break by the lake! And since Velma's car is out of action now, I'll even lend Mike the British Council car to take you. You'll certainly be better off out of Budapest for now.

STEFAN *(reluctantly)*
You have my number if you think of anything.
And I can ring you. So you may go. Just be careful.

56. EXT. ON THE CAR FERRY
ACROSS LAKE BALATON TO TIHANY.

Lea is standing close to Paul, both looking out over the lake. Afternoon light. They are enjoying the view. Mike Gorman comes over and interrupts the mood.

GORMAN
And *this*, Paul, is where Lakatos proposed building a motorway bridge! I ask you.

PAUL
Instead of the ferry? But the ferry's great!

GORMAN
Not to the dedicated motorist! Thankfully, the whole idea was squashed. Two years ago. But Lakatos lost a lot of credibility. He'd abandoned all his previous principles. People thought he must have been in the pay of the car lobby, or developers —but nobody could ever find any actual developers involved. Bit of a mystery.

LEA *(to Paul)*
But his switching sides put him in favour with the government and big business. That's why he was commissioned to report on the choice between the gas pipelines. But in the old days he would have seen *both* proposals as reactionary, according to his old ecological principles. Precisely the kind of massively destructive technology he had once opposed in the Danube Dam. For what?
Gas, oil, the old interest groups.

PAUL
Well, we're using a car to get here.
Even though there's a train, isn't there?

LEA
Yes, Paul, there's a lovely little train—but not to Béla's place. That's pretty remote. And we *borrowed* a car. I deliberately don't own one—*(changes topic)* Look, we're running late. I'll ring Hugi and ask her to feed us this evening instead of lunch— so we can go straight to Béla's now.

PAUL
Er, so do we skip lunch—?

Lea goes aside to ring Hugi on her mobile phone.
Gorman and Paul looking out over the placid lake.

GORMAN
You know, the real issue of the future is going to be water, not oil—water shortages everywhere. Balaton is the biggest fresh water lake in Europe but the people living round it are being charged more and more to use it.

PAUL
It's privatised? Water water everywhere, and not a drop to drink—unless you pay for it?

GORMAN
More or less. Happening everywhere.
The big private utility companies. Unstoppable.
We'll have to pay to breathe shortly.

LEA *(comes back)*
That's settled. And we can stay over with her tonight, if that's OK?

GORMAN
Fine by me—we can easily get Paul back
in time for his train tomorrow night.

PAUL
No problem. Er, but can I just get a sandwich—
somewhere *en route* to Mr Béla's place?

GORMAN
Mr Rákos. His full name is Rákos Bélay. We just call
him Béla, or Belly, as an old friend. He won't mind if
you do.

57. EXT. RÁKOS'S STUDIO YARD.

Some large ramshackle old buildings surrounding a courtyard full of metal and stone sculptures, scrap metal, miscellaneous objects.
Two barking dogs.
A stream cascades down from the slight hill behind the buildings and feeds into a small pond, which is shaped to look like a miniature Lake Balaton.

The opening viewpoint is from a camera position overlooking the courtyard from a short distance: we can see, but do not hear any dialogue, as Rákos greets Gorman, Paul and Lea.

Rákos is in his 80s but vigorous. Scruffy work-clothes.

The camera tracks Rákos as he gestures at various odd objects in the courtyard. Then he shows them into his workshop.

58. INT. WORKSHOP STUDIO.

As he shows them round the chaotic main workshop, full of various unfinished stone and metal sculptures of several sizes, Rákos is almost indifferent to his work and also answers Paul's questions pretty desultorily. Lea and Gorman inspect the work in the background.

RÁKOS *(to Paul)*
Yes, I did know John Berger in London in the mid-1950s, but only very slightly—and there were a lot of exiled Hungarians around in London then, so the character of Lavin in the novel is a sort of composite—I'm definitely not Lavin. Berger was criticised for implying that his character would have joined the Kadar group rather than fought with the uprising. Well, we all had to make choices. I'm not even sure what Berger's own position was.

PAUL
But you came back? When?

RÁKOS
Very late October '56. I wanted to fight for the rebellion—but I arrived a bit too late, a few days *after* the Soviet tanks rolled in—just in time for the mopping-up operations. I went straight to the Corvin Cinema because somebody told me there was still fighting going on there. There wasn't. Bad timing. I spent six years in prison for that mistake.

PAUL *(gauche)*
Was that, well, awful?

RÁKOS
Actually, it was very interesting being in jail at that time. Almost everybody who eventually ran the Party's cultural apparatus was in jail with me, at least briefly —but when I came out they still banned me from working as a painter or sculptor for twenty years afterwards. But how do you ban an eye? I just collected interestingly shaped pebbles and stones, and played around with them. Made the odd little maquette while working as an engineer. In the factory, I used to weld any left-over bits together. Then I started to make very tiny pieces of very

intricate work that wouldn't even get recognised as sculptures! *(He pulls open a drawer to show lots of tiny and very delicate metal constructions.)* Mere fiddling. Trying out ideas. So the works just happened, ban or no ban.

PAUL
But the ban was eventually lifted?
You could get back to proper work?

RÁKOS
Yes. From '82 to '89 it was a bit easier—I even happened to get known in the West as a 'dissident' artist. So of course I had my own show at the London ICA—*in absentia*. Mainly just large scale photographs, not the works themselves. They gave me an honorary life membership—when I went to London a while ago I was told it had expired!

PAUL
Did you keep in touch with Berger?

RÁKOS
Not really. I did contact John once, when I was planning that recent trip to London. He was living near the Swiss border by then, and we agreed to meet in Geneva. But the coach—I couldn't afford to fly—was running very late, and all I saw of Berger was him standing in Geneva coach station as the bus swept past without stopping. He was waving a baguette and a bottle of wine and shouting "On the way back!" Haven't seen him since. Look, would you all like a coffee or tea?

PAUL *(eagerly)*
Please!

59. EXT. COURTYARD.

Long shot from above as they cross to the house next to the workshop.

60. INT. KITCHEN OF RÁKOS'S HOUSE.

Conversation continues over coffee-making etc.

        RÁKOS *(answering to Paul)*
—Now? Well, it's a lot worse than success. My work is 'in demand', as they say — but not the stuff I really want to do. Since '89 it's the tourists —and the patriotic collectors, the nationalists, who have moved in, but they're just tourists with bigger wallets. They want the same things: they're only interested in myth, legend, national folklore. So I do lots of Hungarian dragons and vampires, and Vlad the Impaler figurines, the original icon of Dracula. It's bad art good, good art bad. And the real blood-suckers, the new vampires, are the ones who made a killing, literally, from the sell-off of all the public assets after '89 and now can afford expensive kitsch. Did you know that it was Bela Lugosi who turned Dracula into a Hungarian instead of a Transylvanian? And Lugosi died in '56 —just as the uprising happened —from drug addiction, morphine, blotting out the pain of reality. I can sympathise. The only decent work I ever get commissioned to do these days is the occasional memorial. I'll probably be asked to do an official one for Emric.

        LEA
But Béla, *why* do you do all this Vlad the Impaler stuff?

        RÁKOS
The money. I have to live. And it pays for the stuff I really do want to do. Which isn't sculpture any more.

GORMAN *(who has been quiet)*
So I guessed, Béla —but *what* is it that you *really* want to do these days?

Rákos falls silent. Pause.

GORMAN
Tell me straight Béla: Why was Emric murdered?

RÁKOS
Ah, Mike, I've been waiting for that question.
Your real reason for coming?

GORMAN
Yes. I've been thinking. Hard.
But I don't have the answers. So come clean.
Was it somehow connected to the Tihany scheme, that crazy abortive road bridge across the Lake.
I see there's a model bridge already installed on your little Balaton pond outside. You supported him, defended him, on that issue—but you must have known it was a complete sell-out to all the interests he had once opposed. But you and he were very close these last couple of years. So: what the hell was going on?

RÁKOS
OK, Mike, Lea. I guess it's time to let the cat out of the bag. A little earlier than we'd planned.
But Emric would want you both to know—
that he hadn't really betrayed anything.
So, let me show you. Yes, you saw my little Balaton Lake—well, think of Heraclitus, and the 39 steps.
(pause)
Let's go outside.

61. EXT. COURTYARD. NOW NEAR DUSK.

They gather at the 'shore' of the miniature Lake Balaton.

RÁKOS
So. All will be revealed—you'll see, literally. Look!

Rákos flicks a switch and several lights come on, including some miniature floodlights around the Balaton pond.

But as Rákos switches the lights on, he is shot. He falls, dead.

62. EXT. ABOVE THE COURTYARD.

Dimitri is perched on a slope overlooking the courtyard — the earlier camera view. He fires a burst from an automatic rifle as he tries to kill them all. Mike, Lea and Paul take cover behind the various stone and metal sculptures in the yard and then manage to retreat inside the main shed. Dimitri and another Russian scramble down from the slope and enter the courtyard in pursuit. They pause outside the workshop shed.

63. INT. WORKSHOP.

Lea, Gorman and Paul take cover behind the larger sculptures and look for defence weapons. Lea finds a nail gun. Gorman a heavy-duty drill. Paul picks up a heavy Vlad the Impaler statuette. They wait.

64. EXT. COURTYARD.

Dimitri and the other Russian are preparing to move into the workshop doorway.

Suddenly, above them a police helicopter arrives, with Stefan and two armed police on board. The helicopter circles but cannot land in the courtyard.

A gun battle as Dimitri fires at the helicopter.
Return fire from the helicopter. Both Russians are shot dead as they try to escape from the yard.

The helicopter flies off to land nearby.

Overhead view: Rákos's body is still by the small Lake Balaton.

65. INT. KITCHEN IN RÁKOS'S HOUSE. LATER.

Stefan, Paul, Gorman, Lea. Grim mood.

      STEFAN *(still plodding)*
Perhaps I should not have taken the risk. I apologise. But none of those explanations seemed right to me. So I had you followed, to see if you really were the targets. We saw too late where the snipers were positioned. And we didn't think Rákos was to be a target. Maybe he was not. It was just poor shooting. But we are still in the dark as to any motive.
(to Gorman:) The photos you took of the car showed the faces very well and several witnesses at the restaurant have identified both the gunmen as having been at the Lakatos shooting, so we know who they were. *(to Paul:)* And we know that it was indeed a set-up, to make it look like a hooligan gone wild—the English boy was, we think, shooting blanks. So it is clear that somebody else actually shot Lakatos, and it must have been a professional hit. But why the Russians wanted to kill Lakatos, we do not know—yet. And now, why kill Rákos Béla? If they meant to? Or any of you?

      LEA
And we don't even understand what Béla was trying to show us. What were we supposed to *see* when he put the lights on? They're still on—but what's supposed to be visible to us? He can't tell us now.

      STEFAN
We will search through this entire place, go through his records, his computer files. We will find a clue. But I am going to give you all an armed escort from now on. Where will you be tonight? Back to Budapest? I can offer you protective custody.

                PAUL *(looks anxious)*
    I though we were going to Lea's grandma's—
    for dinner.

    66. EXT. EVENING. UNDER TRELLISED VINES
    IN THE COURTYARD OF HUGI'S SMALL-HOLDING.

A wooden table is very heavily laden with food and wine. Balmy beautiful evening. It could be an utterly peaceful family gathering in a beautiful setting. Except: there are armed police in the background.

                HUGI *(presiding benevolently)*
            (She toasts them in Hungarian—she has no English.)
    Üdvözlöm! Az Ön egészsége! Egészségére!

                LEA   *(to Paul)*
    Hugi has prepared a local speciality for you.
    It's traditionally cooked over a charcoal fire —
    it's called the 'fogas', a sort of pike or perch, unique
    to Lake Balaton. And the wine is Tokaj Aszú,
    'the king of wines and the wine of kings.' Now: eat!

Slow overlap dissolve to: the same scene, but the meal has ended. Paul is finally no longer hungry and all the plates are almost empty.

                HUGI *(to Lea)*
    Eszik sokat. Ő egy helyes magyar!

(Gorman laughs.)

                PAUL
    What did she say?

                LEA *(smiles at him)*
    Hugi likes you. She says you eat well,
    you are a proper Hungarian!

PAUL
Please thank your grandmother—and please tell her I was really hungry! Köszönöm. Egészségére!

ALL:
Egészségére!

GORMAN *(quietly)*
To absent friends.

They drink a toast. Fade.

67. EXT. HUGI'S COURTYARD. MORNING LIGHT.

Written:] WEDNESDAY

The table is laid for a generous breakfast. Paul and Lea are drinking coffee. Relaxed.

LEA
We could go for a swim in the lake before we leave for Budapest.

PAUL
I think I'd sink! I'm still full from last night!

LEA
Well, you could just be lazy and sunbathe. Hugi has a tiny private beach down on the lake. It was Velma's present to her, thanks to Fekete's money. Otherwise, you have to pay for access and so Hugi rarely used to go. She'd be pleased if we used it.

PAUL
Suits me fine. But can we do anything for Hugi while we're here? Any jobs need doing?

LEA
That's kind. Let me ask her.

Lea goes inside, singing happily, in Hungarian:

Föltámadott a tenger,
A népek tengere;
Ijesztve eget-földet,
Szilaj hullámokat vet
Rémítõ ereje.

(Látjátok ezt a táncot?
Halljátok e zenét?
Akik még nem tudtátok,
Most megtanulhatjátok,
Hogyan mulat a nép...)

During this, Gorman comes out of the house and joins Paul at the breakfast table.

GORMAN
Morning, Paul. Sleep well?

PAUL
Fantastic. Never better. It's been a strange few days.

GORMAN
You'll be glad to leave.

PAUL
(listening to Lea singing).
Oh, I'm not so sure. *(pause)* What's Lea singing?

GORMAN
It's a Petőfi poem about the sea—something like :
'The sea is rising up—the people are the sea—its awful power — rises up in great waves'—it was a poem about revolution and the sheer power of the people, like the unstoppable sea.

PAUL
The sea. Ah yes. We were going to go swimming. Do you want to join us?

GORMAN
I might well do. If you don't mind—three's a crowd!

PAUL
Not at all. I'm not sure what's— *(odd pause)*
Sorry, I'm sort of distracted: there's been something
going through my head, and I can't get rid of it.
Maybe it's just that waves poem—Anna quoted me
something like it as well. Rises up in great waves—
The Waves, Lavin's great painting in the novel—
the waves—the wave machine.
(Long pause. Then, excited, shouts:)
Got it!!— "Wave it about!" Wave it about—that's it!

GORMAN *(baffled)*
Woa!

LEA *(comes running)*
What's got into you, Paul!

PAUL *(fast, excited)*
I've just remembered something. Bingo!
When I was talking to Fekete at the Gellert, he took
a phone call from someone — in English—
and at one point he said: Just wave it about.
Just wave it about. It was a gun! Must have been.
When that Inspector was interviewing me—
he said some witnesses at the restaurant shooting
had described the English guy as waving his gun
around, just before the Russian produced his gun.
I bet that's it —it was Fekete who was setting up
the restaurant shooting—but he didn't want Alan to
do any shooting first, since he only had blanks —
in which case it wasn't a feud *between* the Russian
and Hungarian mafia—it was a two-headed
collaboration, they cooked it up together—
to cover the deliberate shooting of Lakatos.

> LEA *(almost amused)*
> A joint enterprise! A Russo-Hungarian venture!

> GORMAN
> So Fekete and Voroshensky are in it together?
> But then why did the Russians shoot at Velma—
> or at Lea? And which one? Was that just a diversion?
> —Hang on. That photo. Just a minute, Paul,
> the photo you took of Velma at the concert.
> Is it still on your mobile phone? Let me look at it—

Paul hands over his phone with the photo on screen.
Gorman examines it closely.

> GORMAN
> Paul, it's wasn't your photographing Velma that
> Fekete was concerned about, but—look!—
> Fekete and Voroshensky are talking together in the
> background of that shot—*That*'s what he thought
> you were photographing—he thought you had
> stumbled onto the connection between him,
> Voroshensky, and the lads from Liverpool—
> which is precisely what you've now done.

> LEA
> —so that means *you* were the target of the shooting
> in the car park, after all, not Velma, or me—

> GORMAN
> I think Lea's right. Look, we need to bring Stefan
> in on this—he's probably still at Béla's.
> I'll ring him, tell him we're coming right over.

68. EXT. RÁKOS'S. COURTYARD

Stefan, Gorman, Paul are talking together , while Lea is wandering distractedly in the background.

STEFAN *(still ponderous)*
You may be right. But we still do not know why they wanted Emric Lakatos, still less Rákos Béla, dead. Or why Fekete and Voroshensky combined to have them killed. And we have not yet found anything at all about the pipeline report in Rákos's papers or his computer. Though he and Lakatos were recently still working together on something they called the Balaton Project. Presumably the road bridge across the Lake.

Lea has been standing looking hard at the miniature Lake Balaton in the courtyard.

LEA
Come over here! Look! *(pause)* Can't you *see*! Those lights are still on, and have been all night. *That*'s what we were supposed to see yesterday when Béla switched them on—the lights, the lights themselves!. Not something we could see *because of* the lights — we were supposed to *see* the lights themselves—that's why he put them on in daylight! Because of what is powering them!

Lea excitedly tracks a thin wire from the array of miniature floodlights to the underside of the model bridge which goes across the lake, and then peers underneath the bridge.

LEA
And *that*'s what's powering them. *(she points).*
My guess is that those small fittings you can just see underneath are tiny hydro-electric turbines—see, under the bridge. A line of them along the whole length of the model bridge— they're so small you can hardly see them—but they're powering those flood-lights, even though the water in the lake is hardly moving. Just the mild in-flow from the stream up there. And *that* shouldn't be *possible*.

She squats down and looks intently around the courtyard.

Then jumps up and runs up to the small stream cascading into the model lake. She starts to trace a cable from a small box at the side of the stream towards the main workshed.

> LEA
> And look at where this goes, to the workshop—
> I bet there's no mains power! It's all powered just from the flow of this small stream. But that's crazy!
>
> GORMAN
> What did Béla say? — think of Heraclitus and the 39 steps. You can't step into the same river twice— and look, count: —there are 39 steps in the cascade.

Lea and Gorman kneel down and peer at the flow of the stream, cascading down across 39 small steps, like an ornamental Renaissance garden water feature.

> LEA *(excited)*
> Each step has a barrier across it, made up of lots and lots of those tiny turbines, through which the water flows as it comes down each step—

Gorman scrambles up to the top of the stream.

> GORMAN
> —And there's not even a stream feeding into the cascade. Just a reservoir, not very big at all. The whole arrangement is a kind of fountain, the water being pumped back up again from the miniature Balaton pond, and so it's actually powering itself again on the way down again. But *that* shouldn't be possible either.
> Not if it's also powering those lights —
> and even the whole workshop at the same time.
>
> LEA
> But it may not be at the same time—maybe the water-pumps work at night, when the workshop doesn't need power—but if there was a constant

stream, even that wouldn't be needed—there would be constant power.

PAUL
Look, I am completely and totally baffled. I'm lost. What is so extraordinary about all this?

GORMAN
Stefan, I know it's early in the morning, but I need a stiff drink. Is there anything in Béla's kitchen that we can raid?

69. EXT. COURTYARD.

Some time later. They are standing around the miniature Lake Balaton. Gorman has a stiff drink in his hand. Stefan is taking careful notes.

LEA *(mainly to Paul)*
OK, I'm beginning to understand what they were up to. You see, the standard way of producing hydro-electric power is that you need a high head drop—the difference in height between the top and the bottom of a waterfall—since it's the force of the falling water that turns the turbines that generate the electricity. So hydro-electric projects normally involve huge turbines powered by the force of a very high head drop, from high reservoirs, or a dam across a major river flow. Like the Danube Dam project which Lakatos opposed back in the '80s. But small head drops produce only small amounts of electricity—every water-mill in a stream is potentially a small-scale hydroelectric turbine—but nobody's ever cracked the problem of scaling up to provide very large amounts of power, except by building larger and larger dams, with higher and higher drops. And more and more expensively.

GORMAN
(he has one of the tiny turbines in the palm of his hand.)
But, look, what Béla had developed are these very *very* small but incredibly super-efficient micro-turbines, like those intricate miniature sculptures he told us he used to make—and these micro turbines look like they can operate on a very small head drop indeed—just the four or five inches of each of those 39 steps in the cascade! But —on the kind of scale he was working on —those 39 steps are the equivalent of a head drop of about 3000 feet!

LEA
And it looks like they can even be turned fast enough just by the flow of slow moving water, like the ones under the model Balaton bridge here. You need a cycle of just 24 rotations per second for standard electricity generation.

PAUL
You mean, like a film, 24 frames a second?

LEA
—But looped, repeated. A continuous cycle. *(pause)* So that's what Lakatos was actually exploring a few years ago—it wasn't really a motorway bridge he wanted built, but the bridge was there to act as a very shallow *dam* across the Lake, which would then be a hydro-electric generator—since, just like the model bridge here, the whole under-side of a full-scale road bridge across the Lake could have had thousands, hundred of thousands, of these tiny turbines suspended from the bridge into the water—

GORMAN
(excitedly using the miniature lake to demonstrate)
And the road bridge across the Lake could also form a storage reservoir, splitting the lake into upper and lower areas with just a small overall drop of a few metres between the two parts of the lake—which

would also allow enough water from the lower area to be pumped back up those few feet to the higher area at night, when demand is low —so that the *same* water falls again the following day and generates yet more power again. Almost like a wave machine which powers itself! Bloody fantastic!

LEA
—Maybe the Balaton road bridge could even have had small step-changes in the flow of water from one side of it to the other—a kind of stepped cross-section— just as the incline of the stream here is broken up into 39 small increments. One of the most controversial aspects of the design was that the bridge wasn't to be raised high above the water level but almost sitting on it—

GORMAN
But if this was going to be possible on Lake Balaton because of its enormous area of water, the biggest lake in Europe, even though it's shallow and slow moving, think of the massive potential for all other kinds of flowing water areas—wherever a micro-turbine barrier could be inserted—even the Gibraltar straits! You could use any part of the entire bloody Mediterranean! Any river! And you don't even need continuous re-cycling of the water either—that was only necessary for the Balaton to act as a constant reservoir as well, like a self-feeding fountain.
I think Béla and Emric had managed to improve the whole design, so they realised they didn't even need the bridge any more—which is why they gave up on that project. Where the water flow is already constant, you could just interrupt it as often as you like, put micro-turbine barriers across again and again. Or just put them out *into* the flow without even stretching right across, since you don't need to create a dam any more. In fact there'd be no need for massive barrages or dams at all, but just a series of micro turbines to slice into the flow again and again.

PAUL *(struggling to follow)*
Like cutting a sausage into segments— but one that sort of joins itself up again and again? What you're saying is that Rákos and Lakatos effectively solved the problem of scaling up—that the micro size of these turbines themselves solves that problem since you can just use them in enormously large quantities —so that instead of huge turbines powered by a very high head drop in one location, blocking a major river, you could have hundreds of thousands of these tiny turbines in a relay or series, with only very small head drops between them—like an ornamental cascade in any part of the river—or even just a distance of flowing water between them—so that each tiny turbine adds its mite of power but altogether they add up to very large amounts of electrical generation. Is that it?

GORMAN
Precisely. The old Stalinist and capitalist mentality was always to do huge things with huge capital investment and so do huge damage to the environment—but now : think small and many, very very tiny and many, many, many—not the enormous Danube Dam of old, but flexible, even portable micro turbines inserted into the stream flow—any section of the Danube could have zillions of these tiny turbines, maybe in something more like a fishermen's net, a micro-turbine in each hole— and these could be serving the local communities along its banks or be fed into a national grid— and not just the Danube, but every other river in the world—think what the Amazon could produce if you needn't even block the river, or dam it up, since the turbines don't need to stretch right across the flow—they can even go *with* the flow in a series or sequence. Basically the break-through was in designing them so small, so elegantly and intricately,

like a delicate sculpture—but also so that they are
cheap to manufacture in very large quantities—
I could make this *(the turbine in his hand)* for a few
pence.

    STEFAN *(pouring cold water)*
Yes, 'bloody fantastic.' Or just fantasy. *Do* they work?.
Please calm down. We did find some designs on the
computer for what look like these turbines—but we
couldn't see how they were connected to the murders.
I think I now get the bigger picture. And I can see why
certain interests might not want such a development.
Lakatos knew that *if* Béla's turbines actually worked—
then the logic of that would be for him to recommend
rejection of *both* pipelines—if these turbine things were
sufficiently fast and cheap to implement, unlike massive
dam constructions, then the overall demand for
commercial oil and gas would quite soon collapse—
if *any* stretch of water could generate elecricity on a large
scale, you would have the cleanest alternative energy you
could think of—water, water everywhere —but *if* it
worked, a lot of very large energy companies would find
themselves out of pocket. Russian and European,
American and Middle Eastern. Unless they bought all
the rivers and lakes, of course.

    GORMAN
But Lakatos was going to describe Béla's break-
through in his pipeline report to the parliamentary
energy commission, and it would then go public—
it couldn't be suppressed—

    PAUL
So Lakatos and Rákos weren't murdered because of
a competitive feud between rival mafias, but by a
collaboration of oil and gas companies to block this
renewable solution—

STEFAN *(impatiently)*
This technology is all very interesting —
but right now I still need to catch the murderers
of Lakatos and Rákos. And I need to prove it—
and perhaps prevent anyone else from being
murdered to stop this idea coming out. So I have
been thinking. Paul was targetted because they
thought he knew about Fekete's involvement—and
now he does indeed—so perhaps we can use that
knowledge. Paul, I need you, back in Budapest. Will
you help?

PAUL *(plaintively)*
I only came to give a lecture! Is it always like this
when you work for the British Council?

70. INT. STEFAN'S OFFICE. EVENING.

STEFAN
Paul, you know what you have to say—and in your
best Liverpudlian accent, please. I know they all
sound the same, but we need to convince Fekete.

Paul rings a number on his mobile phone. We hear only his side of the conversation. Stefan is listening in and recording.

PAUL *(in heavy Liverpudlian accent)*
That Mr Fekete?—Yeah, we've met. —Ah, but *I*
know who *you* are. — And you owe me and my
mates *money*. Well, those of us who are, like, still
around to collect it. An' I reckon you now owe us
a shit of a *lot* of money. — Yeah, well, listen—that
was a pretty big fish you fried the other night. And
the price of fish has gone up, like. —I'd say, about
ten times—yeah, inflation's bad this year, y'know.
— *And* I *can* get a better price, elsewhere — That
sounds more like it. Tomorrow, then. — No, I call
the shots. —Twelve noon, at the bottom of that
funny fernicular thingie that goes up the hill. —

Yeah, and no funny business. Cos it won't be just me. Some of my mates are still here, y'know. So, I'll see ya tomorra. With the cash.

> STEFAN *(highly amused)*
> Well done, Paul! Right, we'll have armed officers inside the fernicular with you. And you'll have bullet-proof protection on. But he won't risk doing anything against you inside the carriage.
> He'd be trapped. So try and make sure we have enough on the wire by the time you get to the top. The conversation just now might even be enough evidence by itself, but it's important, if you can, that you get him to talk about Voroshensky — but we've been through all this. And you're staying here, in protective custody until the operation tomorrow—we can't risk having you on the streets tonight. Don't worry, we can send out for some good food for you! I've even ordered you some cakes from Gerbeaud's —on police expenses. That's a first!

71. EXT. AT THE FERNICULAR RAILWAY. NOON.

Written:] THURSDAY

Paul and Fekete meet at the bottom of the fernicular.

> FEKETE *(recognising Paul)*
> I *knew* you were one of them.

They shuffle on board the fernicular carriage, with two undercover policemen following them on. The carriage slowly ascends.

> PAUL *(loudly)*
> So, Mister Fekete, where's me money for keeping me trap shut about, whatsis name, Laxative or something.

FEKETE
(registering curious expressions on the faces of those passengers who understand English)
Keep quiet! You complete idiot, I'm not discussing it here! I just needed to be sure who you are.

PAUL
Well, I'm certainly me. And people are looking at you, Mister Fekete. Right, you've got till we step off this thingie. And if you don't cough up *now*, I'll shop you *and* Voroshenskiovsky—but I'll make sure Colonel Voroshensky thinks it was *you* that shopped *him*. How would that suit, eh? Fancy the Ruskies getting after you, eh, Fekete?

FEKETE
(panicking as he thinks Paul is going to blurt out the details)
You don't think I'd bring it with me, do you! And I've already told Voroshensky about you. So don't try to play us off against each other. I'll pay you. And that's it.

PAUL
So where is it, then? Come on, cough up, Fekete.

FEKETE
(appalled at the way Paul is speaking openly) Will you shut up! Look, all I can give you right now is a bankers draft. But I have to authorise it before you can cash it. So I have to call my bank.

PAUL
A fuckin' cheque. Thought we were in Hungary! Do it right now then.

FEKETE
(he makes a call on his mobile phone, in Hungarian:) Igen. Ott áll a bal oldalamon. Kék kabát. Jeans. Adj időt.
(Yes. He's standing on my left. Blue jacket. Jeans. Give me time.)

72. EXT. OVERLOOKING THE FERNICULAR EXIT.

A gunman is waiting, hidden, listening on a mobile phone.

73. EXT. NEAR THE FERNICULAR EXIT.

Stefan is listening in to the wire on Paul and hears Fekete's message. He frowns. Urgently uses his radio to alert several undercover men to keep their eyes peeled—

The fernicular slowly reaches the top.
As Paul and Fekete leave the carriage,
the hidden gunman shoots—
but deliberately shoots Fekete first, who falls dead.
As the gunman lines up a second shot, on Paul,
he is himself shot by an undercover policeman.

Stefan rushes to Paul, who is looking scared.

> STEFAN
> Sorry, Paul, I really didn't think that was likely—but you had the protection jacket on. You would have been OK—they always aim at the chest.

Paul loks down at Fekete, shot very cleanly through the forehead.

> PAUL
> Is that so?

74. EXT. GEORGY'S RESTAURANT.
BALMY EVENING.

At a table in the pavement area, Paul and Lea, Gábor and Anna, Gorman and Hugi, Andrew and Stefan, waiting for a huge dinner order to arrive.

Stefan has a laptop with him. He shows Lea the detailed plans of the turbines. She continues examining them closely while Stefan explains to the rest:

> STEFAN
> So, the immediate trail is closed. Colonel Voroshensky has claimed diplomatic immunity and has left Hungary —though our Russian Embassy contacts say he was really working for the Russian oil oligarchy not for the government. If there's a difference. And with Fekete's death we're not sure we can trace who was really employing them both. Most probably a collaboration between Western and Russian oil and gas interests.

> GORMAN
> There's one loose end that puzzles me. How did Fekete and Voroshensky, or whoever they were working for, get to know about Béla's turbines in the first place?

> STEFAN
> The files on Rakos's computer indicate that at one point he and Lakatos experimented with very low-level wave power, using Hugi's small private beach, the one Velma bought for her. So we think that Velma may have stumbled across their set-up and mentioned something to Fekete. Perhaps he went and saw it, and realised what might be involved. Any rate, I'm going to see Velma tonight, to check if that was what did happen—so I won't join you for the meal. *(Unexpectedly, he smiles very broadly)* After all, Velma is now a very attractive and wealthy widow—and she might even want to switch sides in the endless war on crime— You never know.
> Any rate, Paul, when are you leaving Budapest?

PAUL *(looking at Lea)*
I'm not sure. I might be staying for a while, after all.

LEA *(completely preoccupied with the laptop)*
—Look, these designs are brilliant but simple—basically, the tiny turbines are Venturi designs, but with a very fine two-slit arrangement reinforcing an overlap wave-pattern, then combined into multiple layers—with tiny relays between the magnets, reinforcing electro-magnetic resonances at each turbine segment—brilliant—we just have to make sure these go public—we have to get these design specs up on the internet so that anybody can freely manufacture them—

STEFAN
Lea, can I have my laptop back please. And perhaps right now you might have other things—

Interrupted by the arrival of Georgy and waiters with a huge meal.

LEA
Ah, yes, food!

GÁBOR *(a toast)*
Egészségére! Cheers. Eat well!

PAUL
I'm not sure I can—I'm still full from Hugi's meal two nights ago.

Sudden raucous shouts of "Everton! Everton!" from somewhere down the street.

Paul pauses with the first bite half-way to his mouth.

Freeze.

The End.

Printed in Germany
by Amazon Distribution
GmbH, Leipzig